Dulcimer à la Mode

Arranged by Lorinda Jones

Online Audio www.melbay.com/20105BCDEB

Audio Contents

1	DAA Tuning Notes-Ionian Mode	13	DAG Tuning Notes-Mixolydian Mode
2	Rosewood Casket	14	Hurree, Hooroo
3	Bendemeer's Stream	15	Rock-A-My Soul
4	Careless Love	16	Little Maggie
5	Flow Gently, Sweet Afton	17	Over the Waterfall
6	Burden Down	18	June Apple
7	DAG Tuning Notes-Dorian Mode	19	DAG Tuning Notes-Aeolian Mode
8	Cluck Old Hen	20	Butcher Boy
9	Pretty Polly	21	Nine Hundred Miles
10	Scarborough Fair	22	Wayfaring Stranger
11	Drunken Sailor	23	Bound for the Promised Land
12	She's Like a Swallow	24	Shady Grove

The companion audio provides tuning notes for each of the 4 modes and presents each song played through twice. There is a slight pause between the "melody only" and the "melody with accompaniment" arrangement.

I0806879

1 2 3 4 5 6 7 8 9 0

Visit us on the Web at www.melbay.com — E-mail us at email@melbay.com

About this book:

When I began playing the mountain dulcimer, I often heard the dulcimer referred to as a "modal instrument." I vaguely remembered studying the modal scales in my music theory classes, but had not made a practical application of the knowledge. Through reading, workshops, and my own study of the dulcimer, I learned I had nothing to fear, but rather an easy way to learn the variety of scales that are played by musicians of all genres of music. I hope this book will take the fear away for you as a player and encourage you to retune your dulcimer and take advantage of its versatility. Each tune is presented as a melody with a drone in the mode indicated with strumming and rhythm guides. An optional arrangement, or accompaniment, is also provided for most tunes that employs traditional western harmony with more complex chordal melodies that tend to make the melodies reflect less of the ancient modal sound and more of western style harmonization. The companion audio reflects each tune as found in the tablature, along with a simple accompaniment for your practice and listening pleasure.

Arranged by:
Lorinda Jones
PO Box 123
Rineyville, KY 40162-0123
Losnotes@infionline.net

Edited by:
Joyce Ochs
Louisville, Kentucky

A big thanks to the time and effort put forth by Joyce in editing this book. You may still find an incorrect word, fret number, or music note, but thanks to Joyce, you will have a harder time finding them.
Thank you, Joyce!

Other Mountain Dulcimer Publications by Lorinda Jones

Learn To Play The Mountain Dulcimer, Books I and II, Instructional guide to playing the mountain dulcimer
Lullabies and Other Lilting Melodies, Book and Audio
The Celtic Collection, Book and Audio

Recordings

Night Cap, Celtic and American folk melodies performed on Celtic harp, mountain/hammered dulcimer, and a variety of string and wind instruments, 1997 Publication
A MidWinter's Feast, Traditional Christmas and seasonal tunes arranged for traditional strings and winds, 1998
Cottages and Castles, Celtic songs, airs, and dances arranged for mountain and hammered dulcimers, harp, tin whistle, guitar, mandolin, violin, oboe, English horn, 2000 Publication
No Shadows, Solo and ensemble tunes featuring the mountain dulcimer. Traditional American and Celtic. 2002

Table of Contents

What is a mode?

A mode is a scale of seven different tones progressing by half or whole steps to each note (tone) in the scale. The order of these whole steps and half steps identify the specific seven modes in which the ancient Greeks mathematically worked out and established in the sixth century B.C. **The Ionian, Dorian, Phrygian, Lydian, Mixolydian, Aeolian, and Lochrian** modes were named after people inhabiting Asia Minor. There are many fine publications available that study the modes in depth. The aim of this publication, however, is to introduce the four most common modes heard in Appalachian music and suggest songs, tunings, and arrangements for each of these. It is NOT a comprehensive guide to modal scale study.

Where is a mode?

If you look at your dulcimer fret board, without a 6 1/2 or 1 1/2 fret, then the scale structures are easy to see. The **Ionian** mode is the scale that has become our most common "major scale" of today. The correct alignment of half and whole steps begin on fret "3" and end on "10" to complete one octave. (Imagine the white notes of the piano from "c" to " c" .)

Fret:	3		4		5		6		7		8		9		10
Interval:		whole		whole		half		whole		whole		whole		half	
Solfege:	DO		RE		MI		FA		SOL		LA		TI		DO

The next closest related mode is similar to the above major scale, but has a lowered 7th degree. The **Mixolydian** mode begins on open string and ends on "7". (Imagine "g" to "g" on the piano)

Fret:	0		1		2		3		4		5		**6**		7
Interval:		whole		whole		half		whole		whole		**half**		whole	
Solfege:	DO		RE		MI		FA		SOL		LA		**TE**		DO

The **Dorian** mode begins on fret "4", ends of "11", and has a minor scale sound, with a "raised 6th degree," having a more haunting sound. (Imagine "d" to "d" notes on the piano)

Fret:	4		5		**6**		7		8		9		**10**		11
Interval:		whole		**half**		whole		whole		whole		**half**		whole	
Solfege:	LA		TI		DO		RE		MI		FI		SOL		LA

Another minor sounding mode is the **Aeolian**, beginning on fret "1", and ending on fret "8". This is sometimes referred to as the natural minor scale. (Imagine "a" to "a" notes on the piano)

Fret:	1		2		**3**		4		5		**6**		**7**		8
Interval:		whole		**half**		whole		whole		**half**		**whole**		whole	
Solfege:	LA		TI		DO		RE		MI		FA		SOL		LA

4 MODES FOR THE DULCIMER

IONIAN TUNING (DAA)

Do Re Mi Fa Sol La Ti Do
3 4 5 6 7 8 9 10

DORIAN TUNING (DAG)

Do Re Mi(flat) Fa Sol La Ti(flat) Do
4 5 6 7 8 9 10 11

MIXOLYDIAN TUNING (DAD)

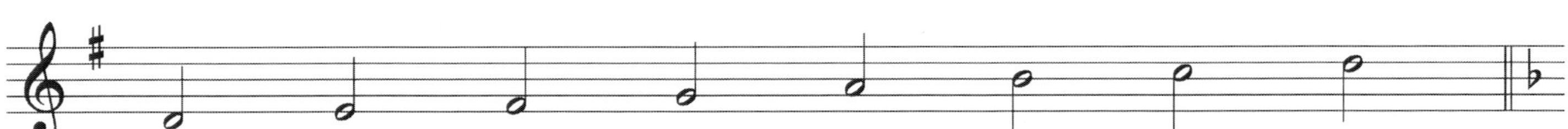

Do Re Mi Fa Sol La Ti(flat) Do
0 1 2 3 4 5 6 7

AEOLIAN TUNING (DAC)

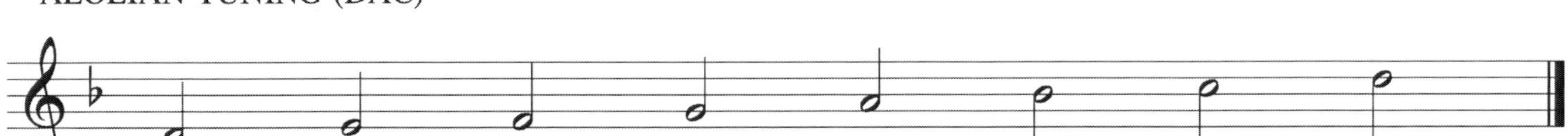

Do Re Mi(flat) Fa Sol La(flat) Ti(flat) Do
1 2 3 4 5 6 7 8

How do I retune for each mode?

For a "D" mode, or scale, leave your bass and middle string tuned in the D-A drone, an interval of a fifth, and change only your treble, or melody string(s). For the tunes in this book, tune your bass string to "d", your middle string to "a" and your melody string(s) to:

Mode	*bass*	*middle*	*melody*
D Ionian	**d**	**a**	**a(fret bass string on 4)**
D Dorian	**d**	**a**	**g(fret bass string on 3)**
D Mixolydian	**d**	**a**	**d(fret bass string on 7)**
D Aeolian	**d**	**a**	**c(fret bass string on 6)**

(each section of the book will walk you through this process)

When you retune the melody string, fret the bass string on the fret suggested to hear the sound of the note you are listening for on the melody string. With each retuning, you will now find chord positions have changed. This is the beauty and challenge of retuning your dulcimer, as you have now extended the possibilities of chord configurations.

How To Use The Charts and Symbols In This Book

4 MODES FOR THE DULCIMER (page 5)

The modal scales used in this book are represented on music staff with appropriate fret numbers, and solfege syllables underneath each note. This shows that each scale will begin on the note "d", when tuned as suggested, and each scale has its own particular key signature, as shown at the beginning of the staff lines.

NOTE MEMBERS OF THE COMMON CHORDS FOUND IN 4 MODES (page 10)

If you decide to find your own chords from the fretboard map, you will need to know what notes make up each chord you are playing. This page identifies the notes that are found in each chord, written underneath the staff representation of the notes. The major and minor chords only require 3 notes, the 7th chords are made up of 4 notes. On a 3-string dulcimer, one of these notes is left out in forming the chord, often the root, or fifth degree. You can also double a note in the major or minor chords, but the chord will not sound as identifiable as when all 3 notes are present.

NOTES ON THE FRETBOARD (page 8-9)

These are the notes that sound at each fret, for each tuning in the book. They are grouped together by either "Major Tunings," or "Minor Tunings." Use this chart to find a particular note, either for melody playing, or chord making.

Ready-made chord options in 3 positions (page 11-13)

Beneath each stated tuning, the most commonly used chords in that tuning are presented in 3 positions to give you options for playing chords in the low, middle, and high range of your instrument. The chord symbols are at the top, with the scale degrees that each chord is built on, directly below the chord symbol. The scale degrees that naturally form a major chord in the specific mode is in capitol Roman numerals, (I, IV, V, V7 for example) and the scale degrees that naturally form a minor chord in that mode is written in lowercase Roman numerals, (ii, vi for example).

All chords in the chart, and in the song selections, are listed from the BASS string to the treble string, in that order. The chords most often used in the LOW position are repeated again at the beginning of each section, along with the complete chord positions. You are given permission to copy, laminate, and cut and use these pages for a quick reference when playing in the various tunings. (page 11)

SONG SECTION

Most songs are presented first as a melody on the treble string only, along with song lyrics, when applicable, and aids in playing the rhythm as notated. The bracket that appears underneath a set of numbers or arrows, indicate strumming 2 times on one beat, a "diddy" strum, or an eighth note strum. These 2 notes are twice as fast as the ones not marked. If direction arrows follow a number, it means the number is representing a longer note, and the strums are there to indicate how long to strum before moving on to the next number. Sometimes, numbers are joined together with one arrow. This happens when the note receives part of a count, or is held over, as in syncopated, or dotted rhythms. And finally, if a number appears by itself, strum the number one time, for one beat. Sometimes sections of the music are repeated. This is indicated by a repeat sign (:‖), two dots followed by a double bar line.

NOTE STRUM EQUIVALENTS GUIDE (page 77)

This additional chart is not related to understanding the modes, but rather as an aid in reading the rhythm and related strum suggestions in the tablature. This is a general guide that the mountain dulcimer play can use in translating traditional notation to the mountain dulcimer. It is not a comprehensive study in rhythm, but an overview of the most widely used rhythms in this book.

Thank you for purchasing this guide. Good luck and enjoy retuning!!

Notes on the Fretboard

Major Tunings

Ionian (DAA)

D	E	F♯	G	A	B	C	C♯	D	E	F♯	G	A	B	C	C♯	D
A	B	C♯	D	E	F♯	G	G♯	A	B	C♯	D	E	F♯	G	G♯	A
A	B	C♯	D	E	F♯	G	G♯	A	B	C♯	D	E	F♯	G	G♯	A
0	1	2	3	4	5	6	6+	7	8	9	10	11	12	13	13+	14

Mixolydian (DAD)

D	E	F♯	G	A	B	C	C♯	D	E	F♯	G	A	B	C	C♯	D
A	B	C♯	D	E	F♯	G	G♯	A	B	C♯	D	E	F♯	G	G♯	A
D	E	F♯	G	A	B	C	C♯	D	E	F♯	G	A	B	C	C♯	D
0	1	2	3	4	5	6	6+	7	8	9	10	11	12	13	13+	14

Notes on the Fretboard

Minor Tunings

Aeolian (DAC)

D	E	F♯	G	A	B	C	C♯	D	E	F♯	G	A	B	C	C♯	D
A	B	C♯	D	E	F♯	G	G♯	A	B	C♯	D	E	F♯	G	G♯	A
C	D	E	F	G	A	A♯	B	C	D	E	F	G	A	A♯	B	C
0	1	2	3	4	5	6	6+	7	8	9	10	11	12	13	13+	14

Dorian (DAG)

D	E	F♯	G	A	B	C	C♯	D	E	F♯	G	A	B	C	C♯	D
A	B	C♯	D	E	F♯	G	G♯	A	B	C♯	D	E	F♯	G	G♯	A
G	A	B	C	D	E	F	F♯	G	A	B	C	D	E	F	F♯	G
0	1	2	3	4	5	6	6+	7	8	9	10	11	12	13	13+	14

NOTE MEMBERS OF THE COMMON CHORDS IN BOTH MAJOR AND MINOR MODES

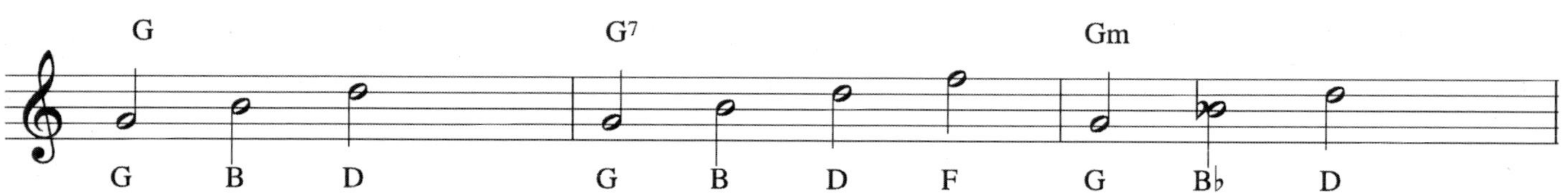

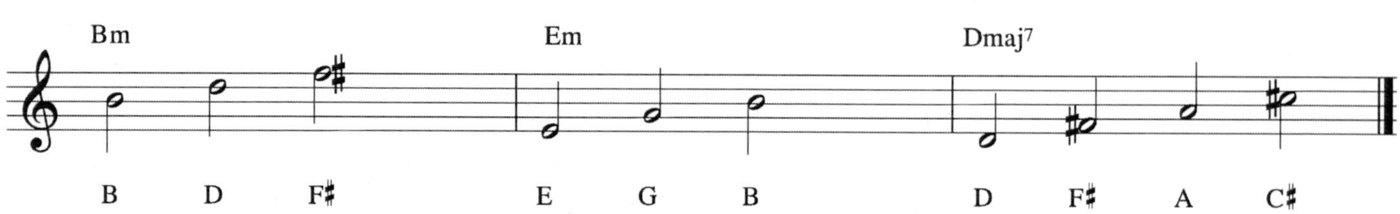

READY-MADE CHORD OPTIONS IN LOW, MEDIUM, AND HIGH POSITIONS IN 4 TUNINGS

DAA TUNING / DAC TUNING

	D	Em	G	A	A7	Bm		Dm	F	Gm	Am	A	C
	I	ii	IV	V	V7	vi		i	III	iv	v	V	VII
D	2	3	3	1	3	2	D	0	4	3	1	4	3
A	0	1	1	0	2	1	A	0	0	3	0	2	4
A	3	4	3	2	0	3	C	3	3	6	0	2	0
D	4	5	5	4	4	5	D	4	6	7	4	6+	8
A	3	4	3	2	2	3	A	3	0	6	4	7	6
A	5	6	6	4	6	5	C	3	3	6	0	9	7
D	7	8	7	8	8	7	D	7	6	10	8	11	13
A	5	6	6	9	6	5	A	7	7	10	7	9	11
A	7	8	8	7	7	8	C	10	10	13	7	9	11

DAD TUNING / DAG TUNING

	D	Em	G	A	A7	Bm		Dm	F	G	Am	A	C
	I	ii	IV	V	V7	vi		i	III	IV	v	V	VII
D	2	3	3	1	1	2	D	0	6	3	1	4	3
A	0	1	1	2	2	1	A	0	0	3	0	2	4
D	0	1	0	4	3	0	G	4	6	2	3	5	3
D	2	3	3	4	6+	2	D	4	6	5	4	6+	6
A	3	4	3	4	6	3	A	3	7	6	4	7	6
D	4	5	5	6+	4	5	G	6	6	4	0	5	5
D	4	5	5	6+	6+	5	G	6	6	4	0	5	5
A	5	6	6	7	6	5	A	7	14	8	7	9	11
D	7	8	7	8	8	7	G	6	13	17	5	8	10

This page may be reproduced, copied, and laminated as a quick guide to chords when playing in the different tunings.

READY-MADE CHORD OPTIONS IN 3 POSITIONS

DAA TUNING

	D	Em	G	A	A7	Bm
	I	ii	IV	V	V7	vi
D	2	3	3	1	3	2
A	0	1	1	0	2	1
A	3	4	3	2	0	3
D	4	5	5	4	4	5
A	3	4	3	2	2	3
A	5	6	6	4	6	5
D	7	8	7	8	8	7
A	5	6	6	9	6	5
A	7	8	8	7	7	8

DAD TUNING

	D	Em	G	A	A7	Bm
	I	ii	IV	V	V7	vi
D	2	3	3	1	1	2
A	0	1	1	2	2	1
D	0	1	0	4	3	0
D	2	3	3	4	6+	2
A	3	4	3	4	6	3
D	4	5	5	6+	4	5
D	4	5	5	6+	6+	5
A	5	6	6	7	6	5
D	7	8	7	8	8	7

DAC TUNING

	Dm i	F III	Gm iv	Am v	A V	C VII
D	0	4	3	1	4	3
A	0	0	3	0	2	4
C	3	3	6	0	2	0
D	4	6	7	4	6+	8
A	3	0	6	4	7	6
C	3	3	6	0	9	7
D	7	6	10	8	11	13
A	7	7	10	7	9	11
C	10	10	13	7	9	11

DAG TUNING

	Dm i	F III	G IV	Am v	A V	C VII
D	0	6	3	1	4	3
A	0	0	3	0	2	4
G	4	6	2	3	5	3
D	4	6	5	4	6+	6
A	3	7	6	4	7	6
G	6	6	4	0	5	5
D	7	13	7	6	8	10
A	7	14	8	7	9	11
G	6	13	7	5	8	10

IONIAN

"Extroverted"

String Tuning: DAA

1. Fret bass string at fret number 4.
Listen to the note and tune melody string to match that pitch.

2. The scale is found between frets 3 and 10 on the melody string.

The character descriptions of each mode:
Ionian "extrovert"

Dorian "bestower of wisdom and chastity"
Mixolydian "awaken"

Aeolian " appeasing the tempests of the mind and lulling them asleep," are attributed to the medieval and Greek theorists.

ACCOMPANYING CHORD POSITIONS IN DAA SONG SECTION

D	G	A	A7	Bm
2	3	1	3	2
0	1	0	2	1
3	3	2	0	3

There are many chords available on the fret board in addition to those listed here. These are some suggested chords used for accompanying in the song section. Check the numbered fret chart for "major tunings", **Ionian**, to create a variety of chords in different position on the fret board.

READY-MADE CHORD OPTIONS IN 3 POSITIONS

DAA TUNING

	D	Em	G	A	A7	Bm
	I	ii	IV	V	V7	vi
D	2	3	3	1	3	2
A	0	1	1	0	2	1
A	3	4	3	2	0	3
D	4	5	5	4	4	5
A	3	4	3	2	2	3
A	5	6	6	4	6	5
D	7	8	7	8	8	7
A	5	6	6	9	6	5
A	7	8	8	7	7	8

Rosewood Casket

Ionian Mode (DAA)

Traditional

2. Go and bring them to me sister
Read them all to me tonight,
I have often tried but I could not,
For the tears that filled my eyes.

3. When I'm dead and in my casket,
When I gently fall asleep,
Fall asleep to wake in heaven,
Dearest sister do not weep.

4. Take the letters and his locket
Place them gently on my breast,
But this golden ring that he gave me,
From my finger never part.

Rosewood Casket

Optional Arrangement

Ionian Mode (DAA)

Traditional

2. Go and bring them to me sister
Read them all to me tonight
I have often tried but I could not,
For the tears that filled my eyes.

3. When I'm dead and in my casket
When I gently fall asleep
Fall asleep to wake in heaven,
Dearest sister do not weep.

4. Take the letters and his locket
Place them gently on my breast,
But this golden ring that he gave me,
From my finger never part.

Bendemeer's Stream

Ionian Mode (DAA)

Thomas Moore

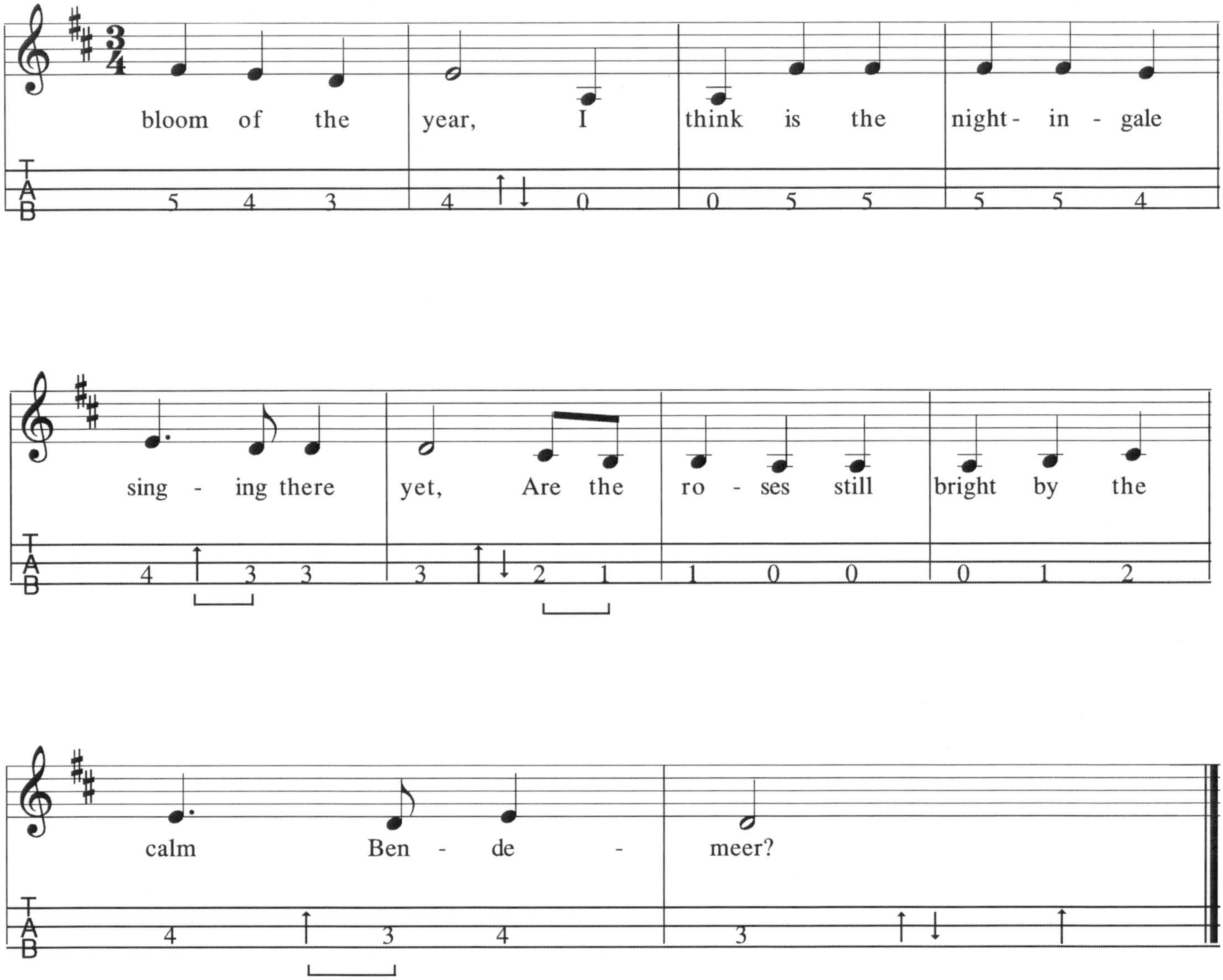
bloom of the year, I think is the night - in - gale
sing - ing there yet, Are the ro - ses still bright by the
calm Ben - de - meer?

Bendemeer's Stream

Optional Arrangement

Ionian Mode (DAA)

Thomas Moore

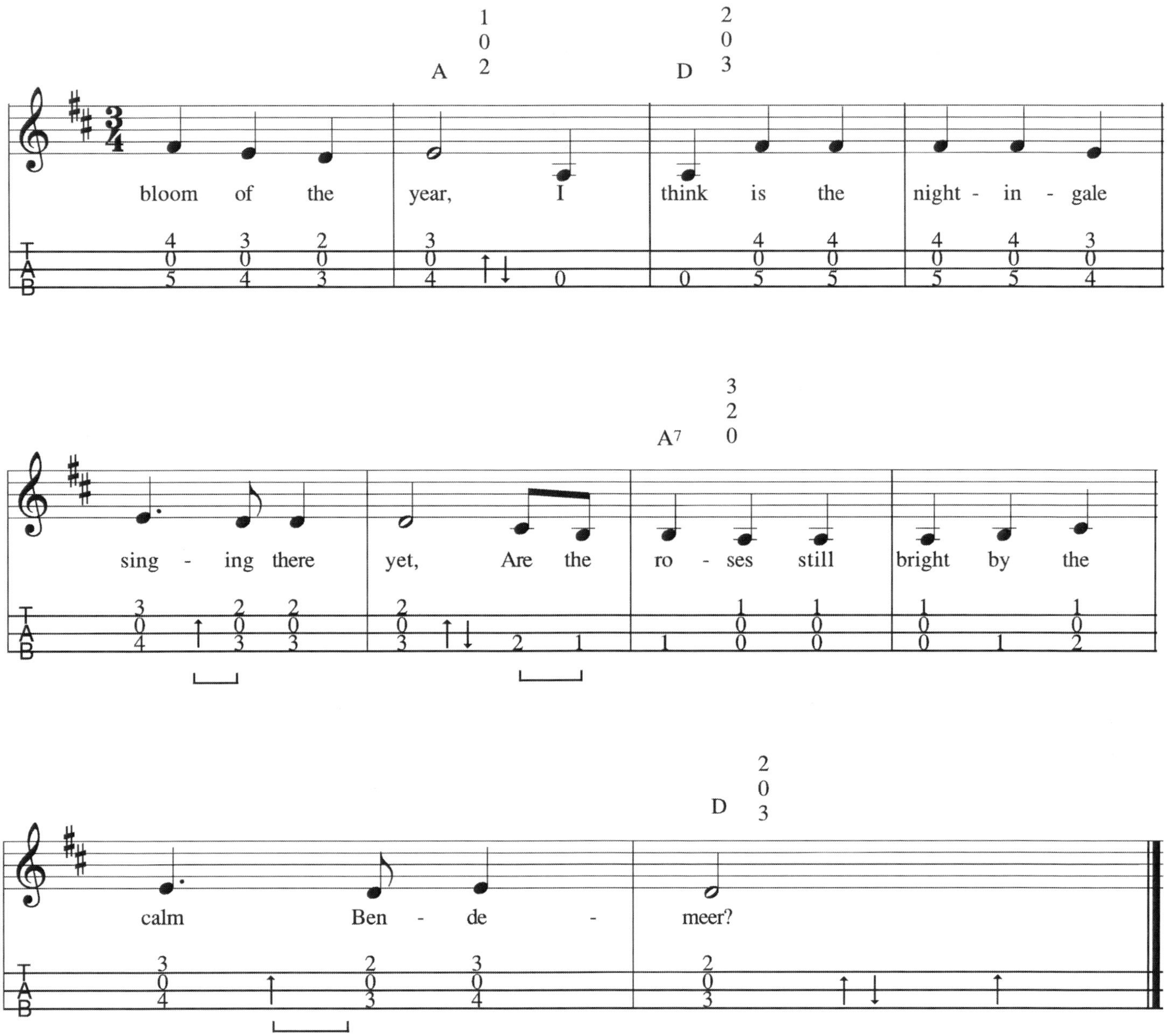
A D
bloom of the year, I think is the night - in - gale
A7
sing - ing there yet, Are the ro - ses still bright by the
D
calm Ben - de - meer?

Careless Love

Ionian Mode (DAA) **Traditional**

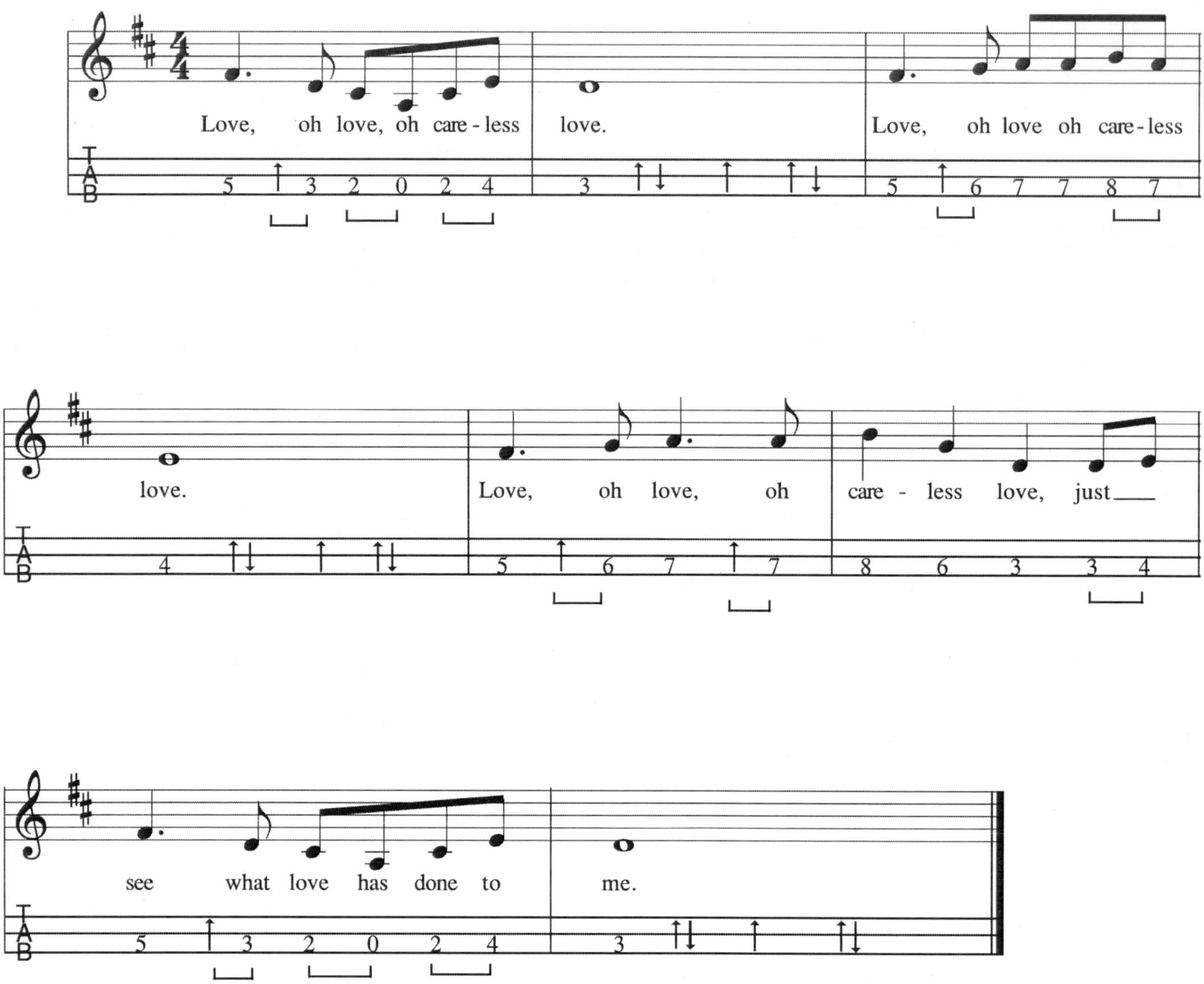

Sorrow, sorrow to my heart
Sorrow, sorrow, to my heart
Sorrow, sorrow, to my heart
When me and my true love must part.

Cried last night and the night before,
Cried last night and the night before,
Cried last night and the night before,
Gonna to cry tonight and I'll cry no more.

It's a pity that we met,
It's a pity that we met,
It's a pity that we met,
For those good times we'll never forget.

Oh, it's broke this heart of mine,
Oh, it's broke this heart of mine,
Oh, it's broke this heart of mine,
It'll break that heart of yours some time.

Careless Love

Optional Arrangement

Ionian Mode (DAA)

Traditional

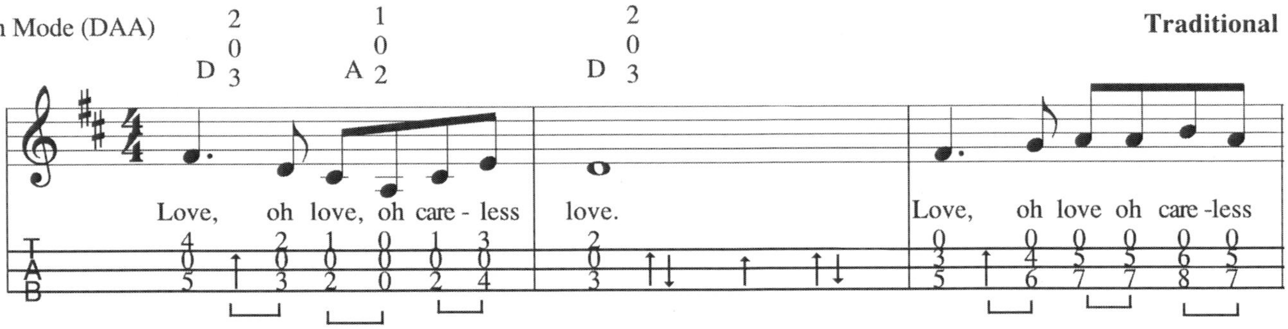

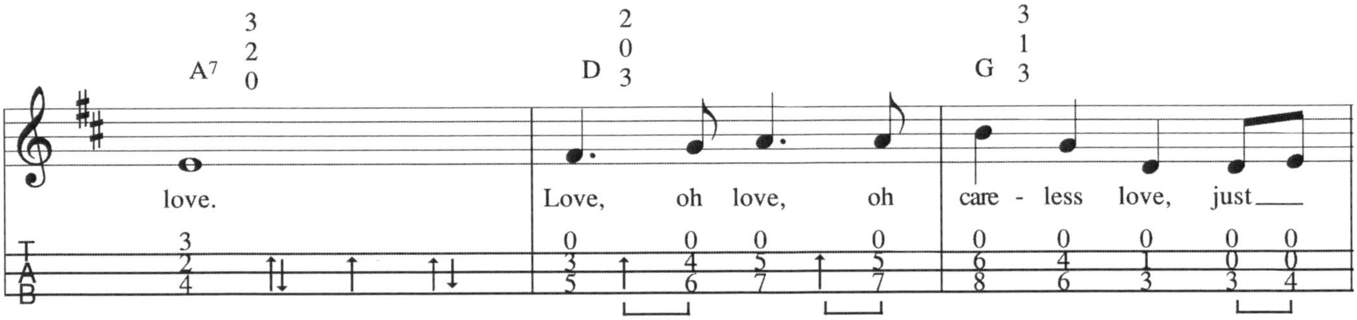

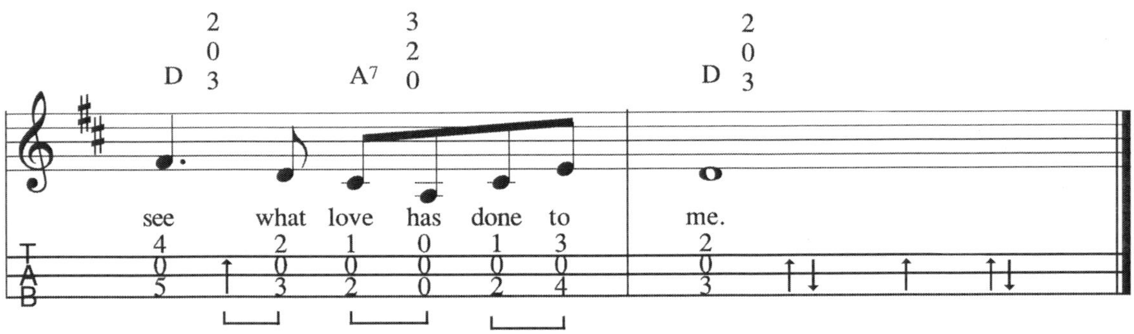

Sorrow, sorrow to my heart
Sorrow, sorrow, to my heart
Sorrow, sorrow, to my heart
When me and my true love must part.

Cried last night and the night before,
Cried last night and the night before,
Cried last night and the night before,
Gonna to cry tonight and I'll cry no more.

It's a pity that we met,
It's a pity that we met,
It's a pity that we met,
For those good times we'll never forget.

Oh, it's broke this heart of mine,
Oh, it's broke this heart of mine,
Oh, it's broke this heart of mine,
It'll break that heart of yours some time.

Flow Gently, Sweet Afton

Ionian Mode (DAA)

Music by Alexander Hume
Words by Robert Burns

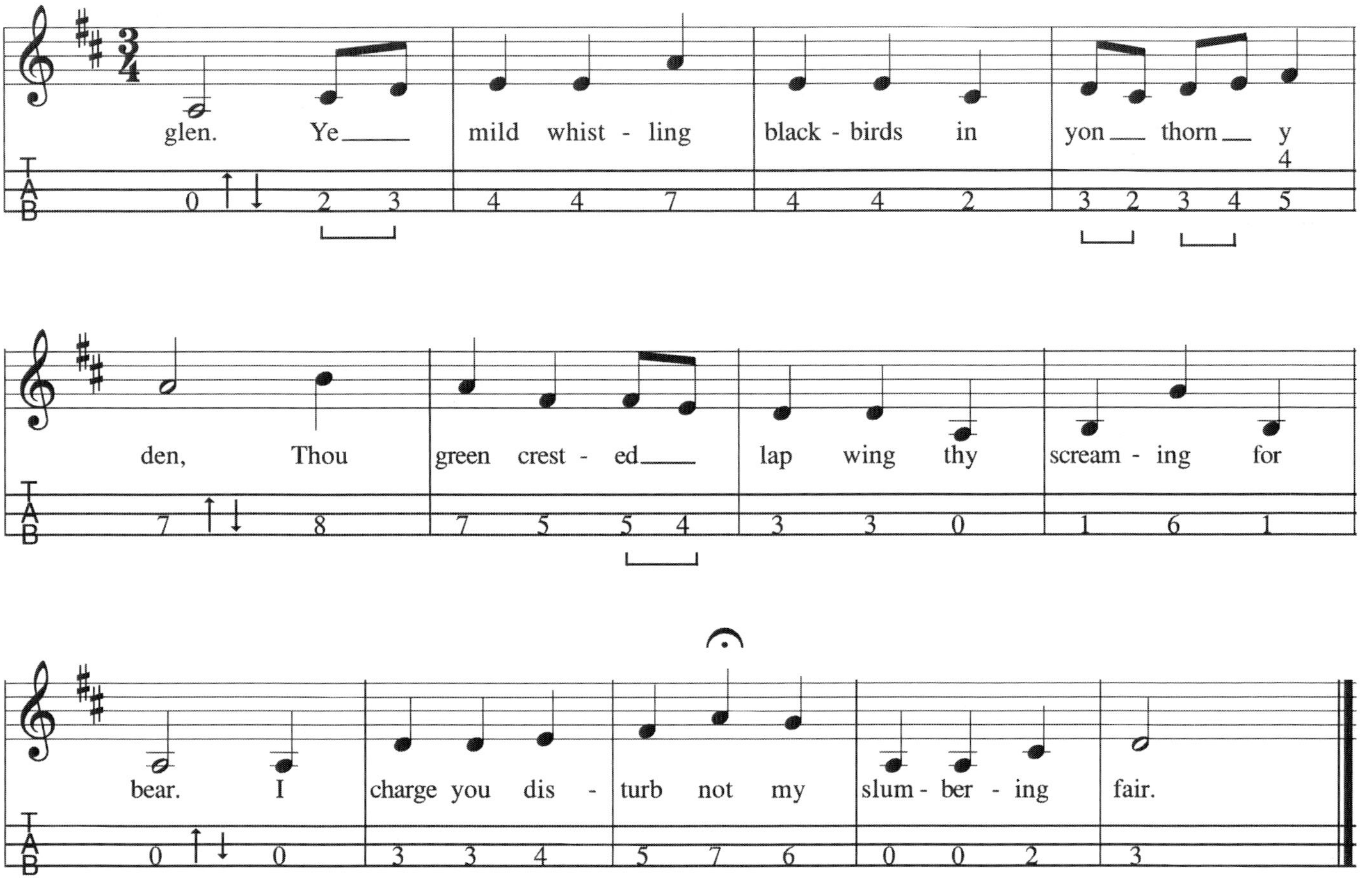
glen. Ye___ mild whist - ling black - birds in yon___ thorn___ y
den, Thou green crest - ed___ lap wing thy scream - ing for
bear. I charge you dis - turb not my slum - ber - ing fair.

Flow Gently, Sweet Afton

Optional Arrangement

Ionian Mode (DAA)

Music by Alexander Hume
Words by Robert Burns

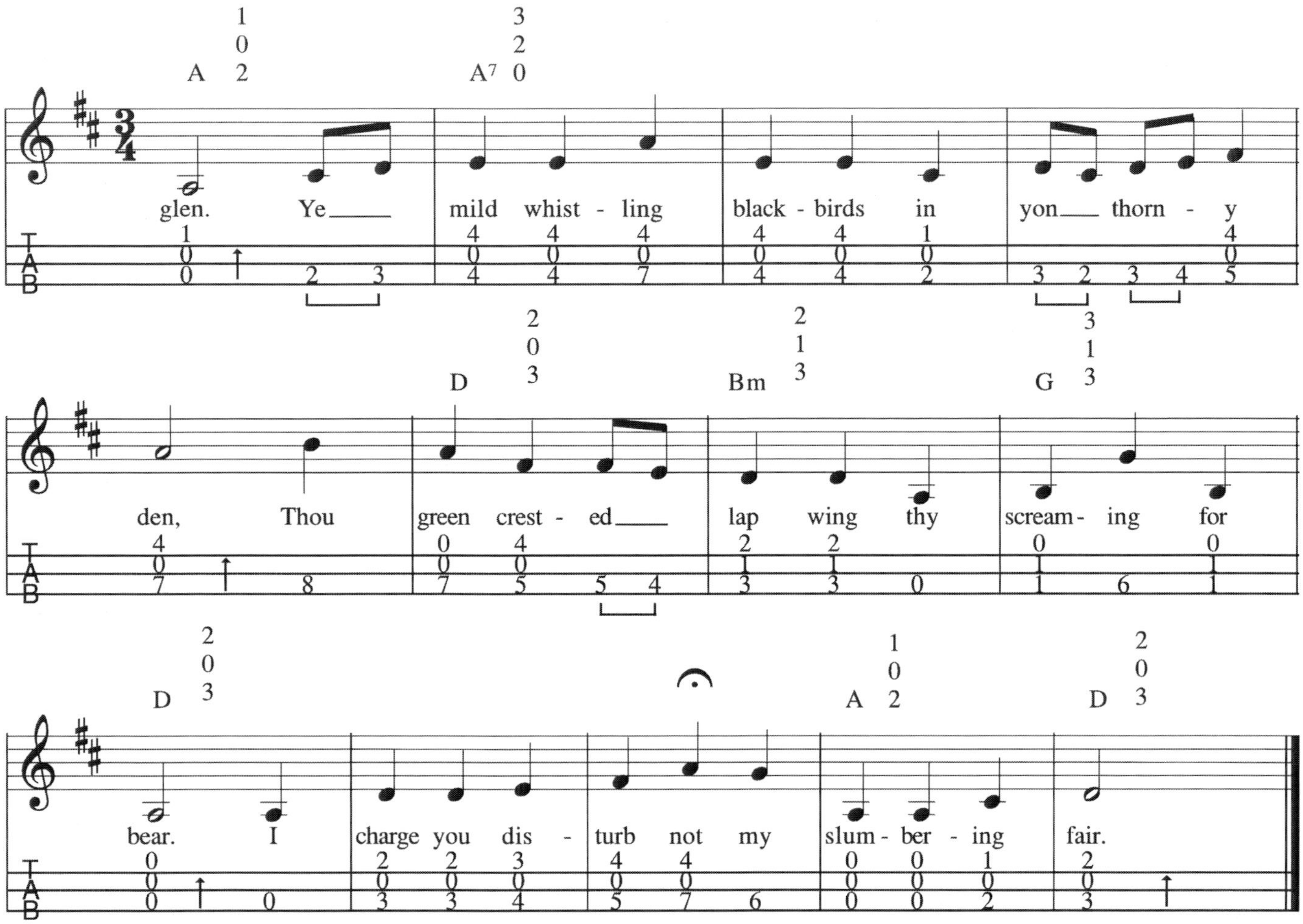
A A7
glen. Ye mild whist - ling black - birds in yon thorn - y
D Bm G
den, Thou green crest - ed lap wing thy scream - ing for
D A D
bear. I charge you dis - turb not my slum - ber - ing fair.

Burden Down

Ionian Mode, DAA

Spiritual

additional verses by Lorinda Jones

I am climbing to the mountain,
Since I lay my burden down,
I am climbing to the mountain,
Since I lay my burden down.

I am walking ever lighter
Since I lay my burden down
I am walking ever lighter
Since I lay my burden down.

Burden Down

Optional Arrangement

Ionian Mode, DAA

Spiritual

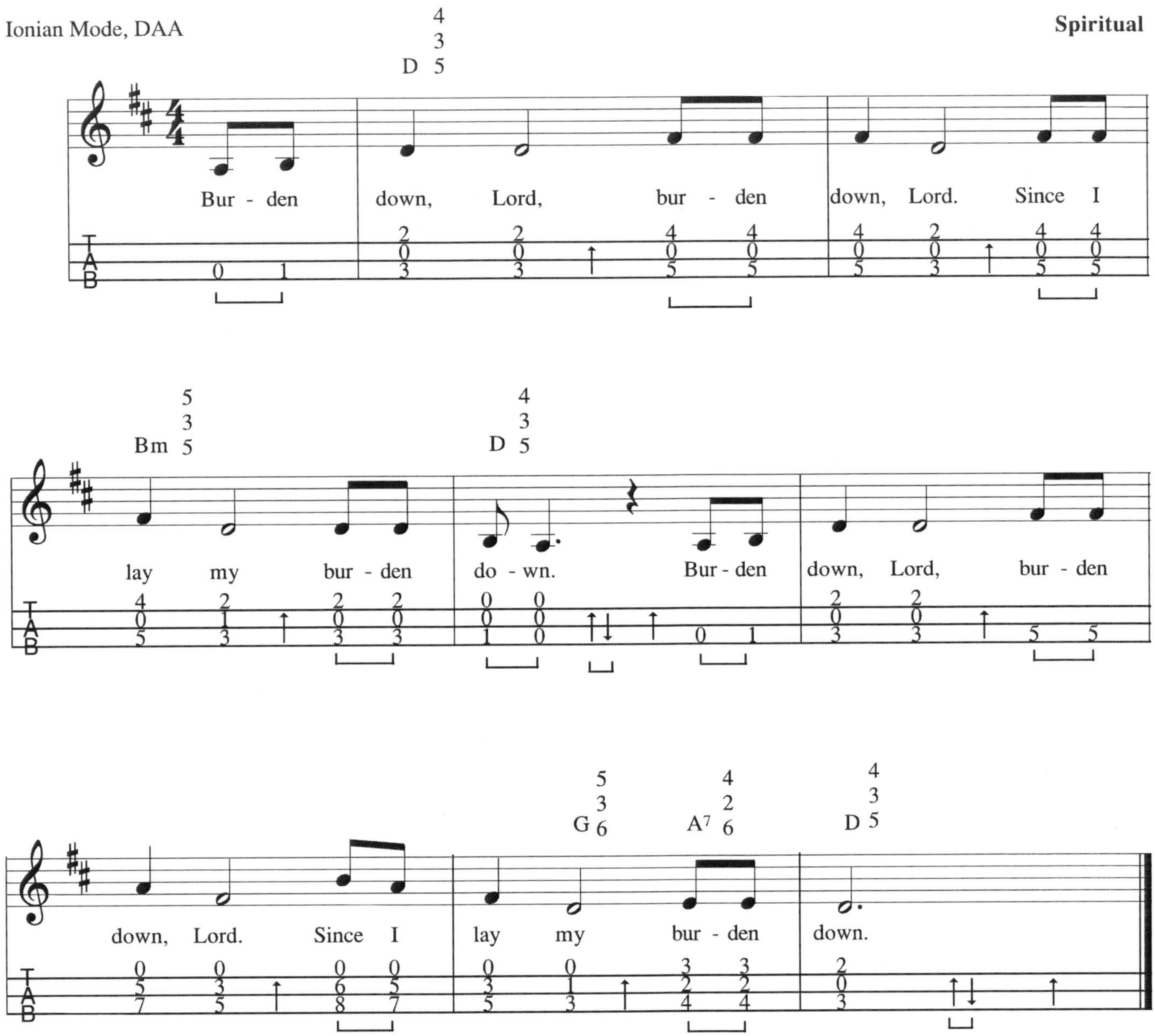

additional verses by Lorinda Jones

I am climbing to the mountain,
Since I lay my burden down,
I am climbing to the mountain,
Since I lay my burden down.

I am walking ever lighter
Since I lay my burden down
I am walking ever lighter
Since I lay my burden down.

DORIAN

"Bestower of wisdom and chastity"

String Tuning: DAG

1. Fret bass string at fret number 3.
Listen to the note and tune the melody string to match that pitch.

2. The scale is found between frets 4 and 11 on the melody string.

ACCOMPANYING CHORD POSITIONS IN DAG SONG SECTION

Dm	F	Am	A7	C
0	6	4	1	3
0	0	4	2	4
4	6	3	0	3

DAG TUNING

	Dm	F	G	Am	A	C
	i	III	IV	v	V	VII
D	0	6	3	1	4	3
A	0	0	3	0	2	4
G	4	6	2	3	5	3
D	4	6	5	4	6+	6
A	3	7	6	4	7	6
G	6	6	4	0	5	5
D	7	13	7	6	8	10
A	7	14	8	7	9	11
G	6	13	7	5	8	10

Cluck Old Hen

Dorian Mode (DAG)

Traditional

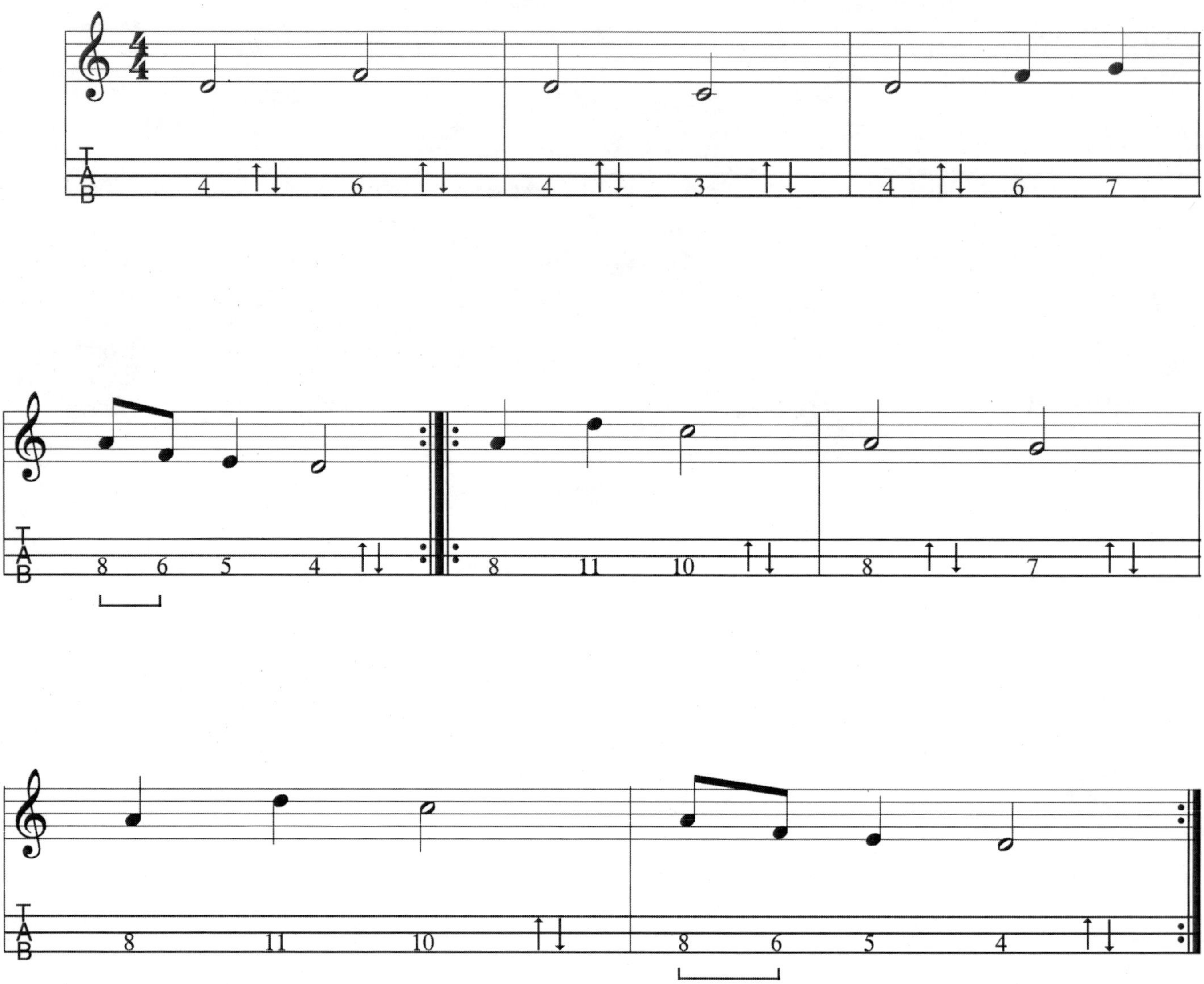

My old hen's a good old hen,
She lays eggs for the railroad men.
Sometimes one, sometimes two
Sometimes enough for the whole darn crew.

My old hen's a good old hen,
She lays eggs for the railroad men.
Sometimes eight, sometimes ten,
That's enough for the railroad men.

Cluck old hen, cluck and sing,
Ain't laid an egg since way last spring.
Cluck old hen, cluck and squall,
Ain't laid an egg since way last fall.

Cluck Old Hen

Optional Arrangement

Dorian Mode (DAG)

Traditional

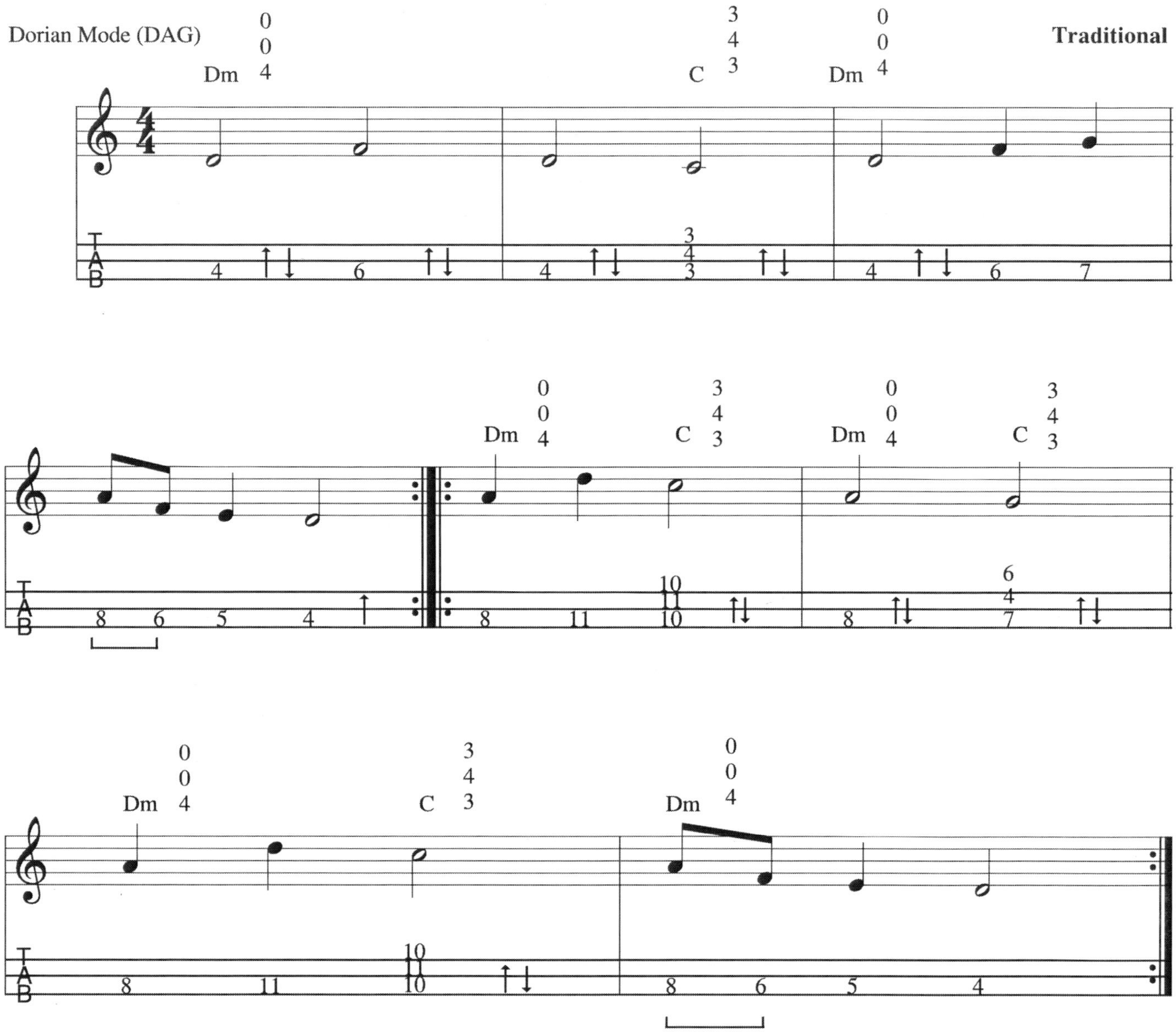

My old hen's a good old hen,
She lays eggs for the railroad men.
Sometimes one, sometimes two
Sometimes enough for the whole darn crew.

Cluck old hen, cluck and sing,
Ain't laid an egg since way last spring.
Cluck old hen, cluck and squall,
Ain't laid an egg since way last fall.

My old hen's a good old hen,
She lays eggs for the railroad men.
Sometimes eight, sometimes ten,
That's enough for the railroad men.

Pretty Polly

Dorial Mode (DAG) **Traditional**

My mind is to marry and never to part
My mind is to marry and never to part
The first time I saw her it wounded my heart

Willie, little Willie, I'm afraid of your ways
Willie, little Willie, I'm afraid of your ways
The way you've been rambling, you'll lead
me astray.

He stabbed her to the heart and the
heart's blood did flow,
He stabbed her to the heart and the
heart's blood did flow,
And into the grave Pretty Polly did go.

He led her over mountains and valleys so deep
He led her over mountains and valleys so deep
Pretty Polly mistrusted and then began to weep

Polly, pretty Polly, you're guessing 'bout right
Polly, pretty Polly, you're guessing 'bout right
I dug on your grave for the best part of last night

He threw the dirt over her and
turned away to go
He threw the dirt over her and
turned away to go
Down to the river where the
deep waters flow.

Pretty Polly

Optional Arrangement

Dorial Mode (DAG)

Traditional

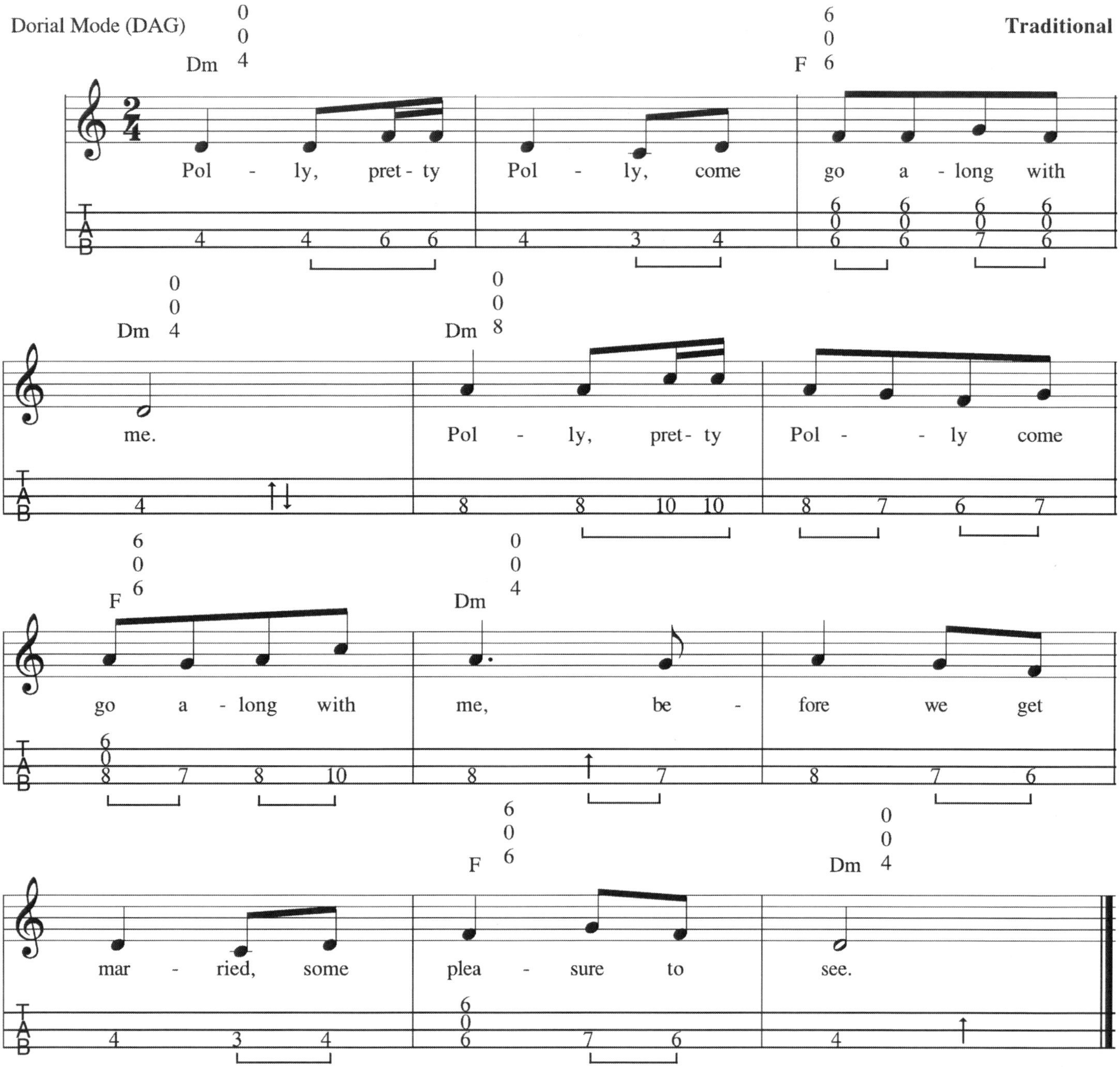

My mind is to marry and never to part
My mind is to marry and never to part
The first time I saw her it wounded my heart.

He led her over mountains and valleys so deep
He led her over mountains and valleys so deep
Pretty Polly mistrusted and then began to weep

Willie, little Willie, I'm afraid of your ways
Willie, little Willie, I'm afraid of your ways
The way you've been rambling, you'll lead me astry.

Polly, pretty Polly, you're guessing 'bout right
Polly, pretty Polly, you're guessing 'bout right.
I dug on your grave for the best part of last night.

He stabbed her to the heart and the heart's blood did flow,
He stabbed her to the hearta and the heart's blood did flow,
And into the grave Pretty Polly did go

He threw the dirt over her and turned away to go
He threw the dirt over her and turned away to go
Down to the river where the deep waters flow.

Scarborough Fair

Dorian Mode (DAG) **Traditional**

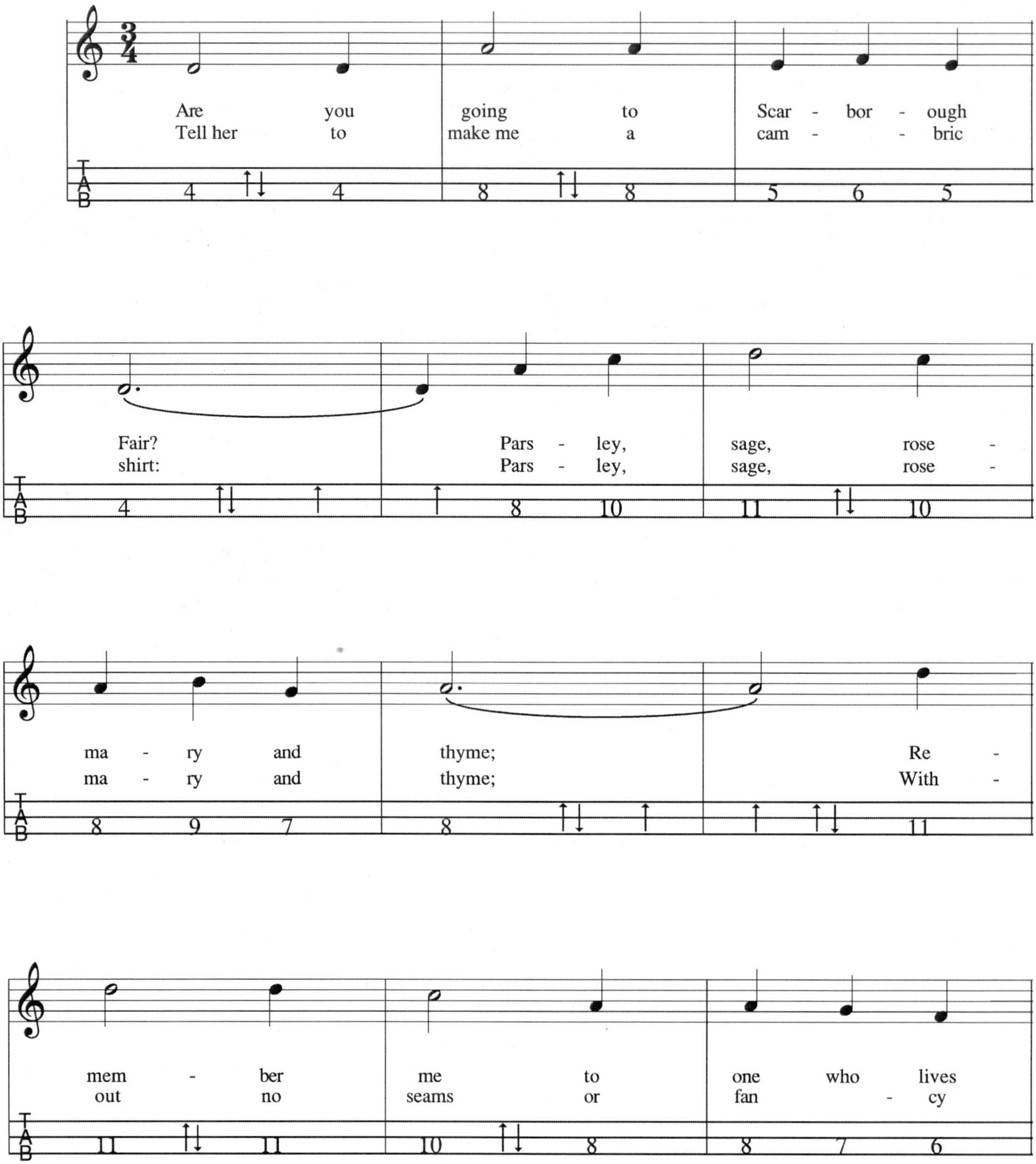

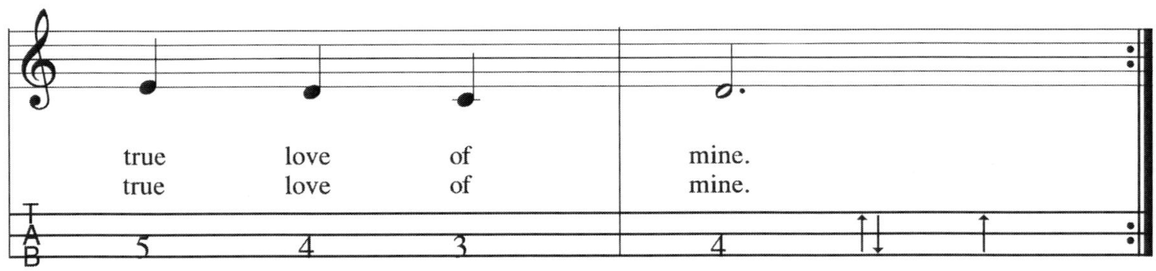

Tell her to wash it in yonder dry well
Where water ne'er sprung nor drop of rain fell

Tell her to dry it on yonder thorn
Which never bore blossom since Adam was born

O will you find me an acre of land
Between the sea foam & the salt sea sand
Or never be

O will you plough it with a ram's horn
And sow it all over with one peppercorn?
& then she'll be

O will you reap it with a sickle of leather
And tie it all up with a peacock's feather?

And when you have done & finished your work
Then come to me for your cambric shirt
& you shall be

Scarborough Fair

with optional accompaniment

Dorian Mode (DAG) **Traditional**

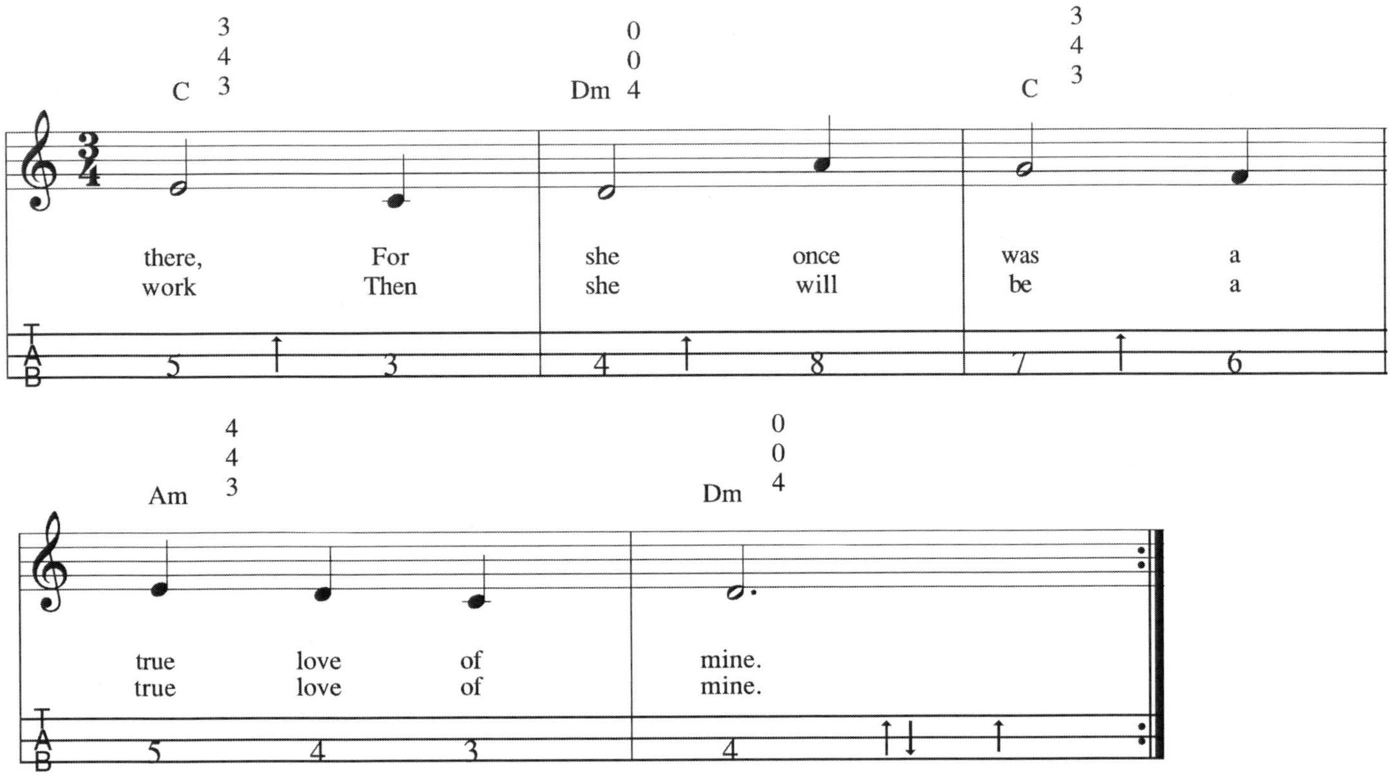

Tell her to wash it in yonder dry well
Where water ne'er sprung nor drop of rain fell

Tell her to dry it on yonder thorn
Which never bore blossom since Adam was born

O will you find me an acre of land
Between the sea foam & the salt sea sand
Or never be

O will you plough it with a ram's horn
And sow it all over with one peppercorn?
& then she'll be

O will you reap it with a sickle of leather
And tie it all up with a peacock's feather?

And when you have done & finished your work
Then come to me for your cambric shirt
& you shall be

Drunken Sailor

Dorian Mode

(DAG)

Traditional

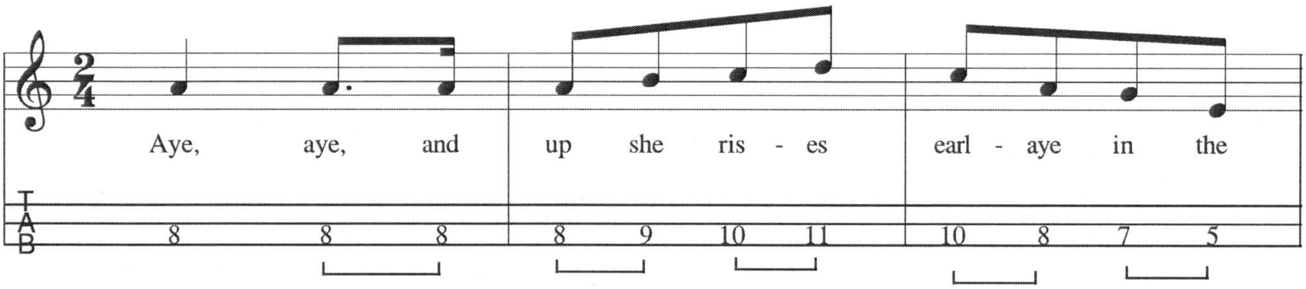

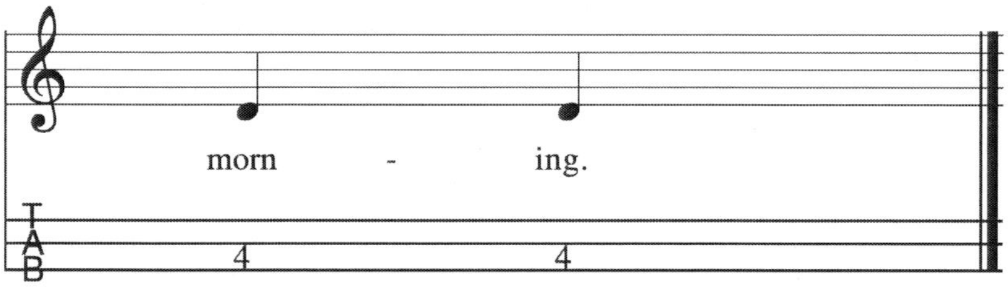

Pull out the plug and wet him all over
Pull out the plug and wet him all over
Pull out the plug and wet him all over
Earl-aye in the morning.

That's what we do with the drunken sailor
That's what we do with the drunken sailor
That's what we do with the drunken sailor
Earl-aye in the morning.

Drunken Sailor

with optional accompaniment

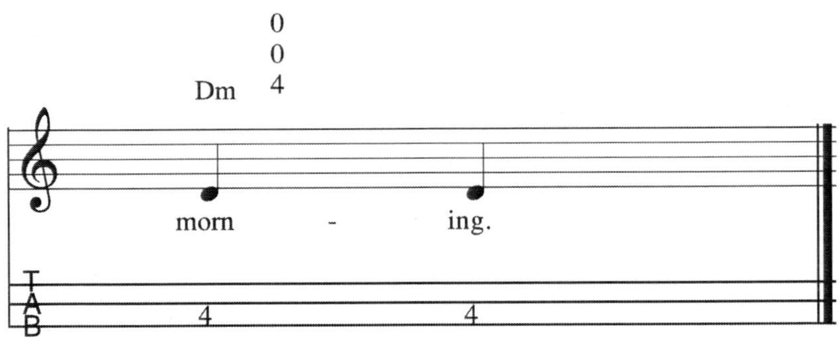

Pull out the plug and wet him all over
Pull out the plug and wet him all over
Pull out the plug and wet him all over
Earl-aye in the morning.

That's what we do with the drunken sailor
That's what we do with the drunken sailor
That's what we do with the drunken sailor
Earl-aye in the morning.

She's Like a Swallow

with optional accompaniment

Dorian Mode (DAG)

Traditional

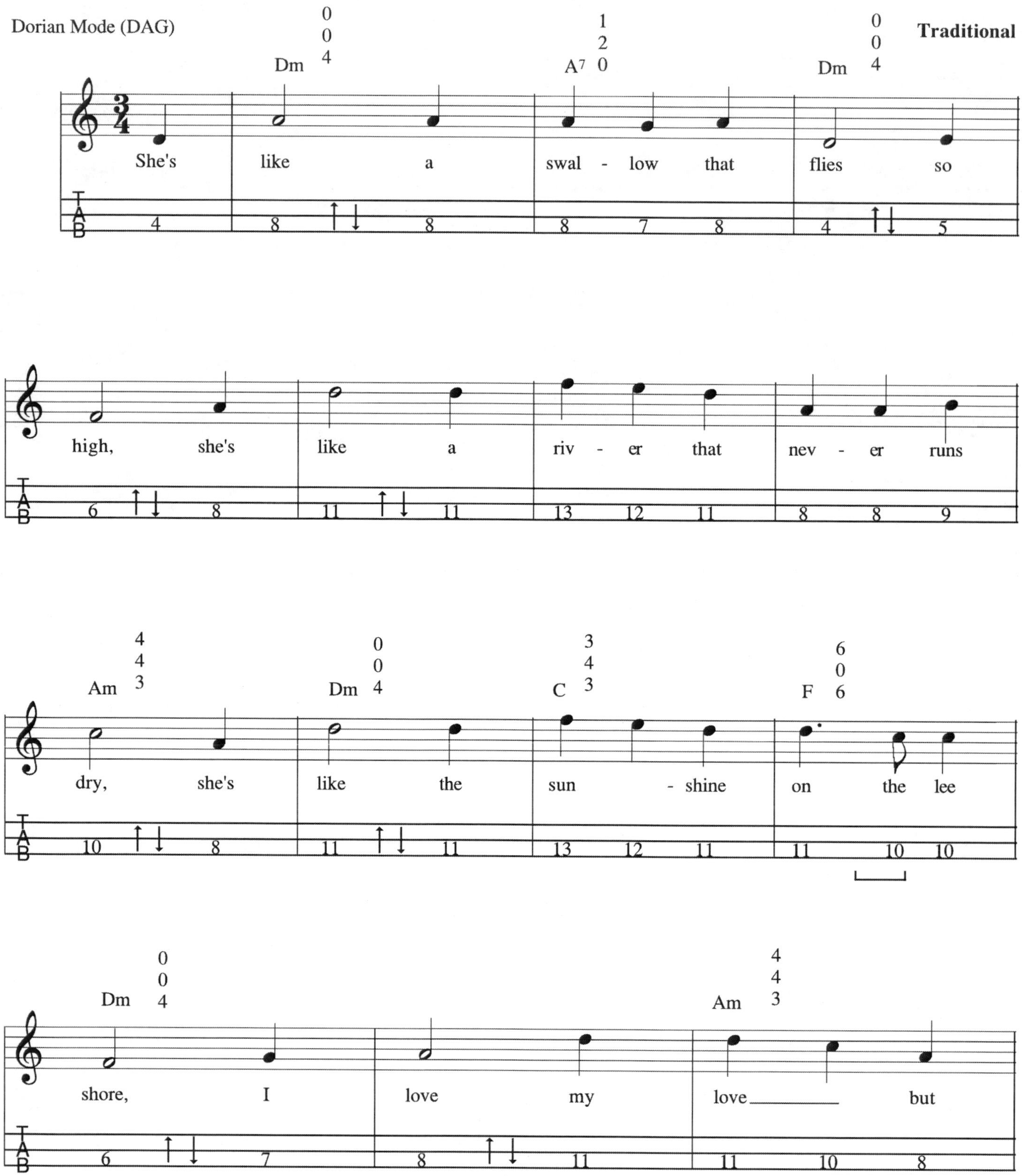

Down to this garden this fair maid did go
To pluck the beautiful prim-rose
The more she plucked, the more she pulled
Until she go her apron full

Then out of these prim-a-roses she made
A thorny pillow for her head
She laid her head down, no word did say,
And then this poor maid's heart did break.

Mixolydian

"Awakening"

String Tuning: DAD

1. Fret bass string at fret number 7, or the middle string at fret number 3. Listen to the note and tune the melody string to match that pitch.

2. The scale is found between frets 0 (open) and 7 on the melody string.

ACCOMPANYING CHORD POSTITION IN DAD SONG SECTION

D	G	A	A7	C
2	3	1	3	3
0	1	0	0	4
0	0	1	1	6

DAD TUNING

	D	Em	G	A	A7	Bm
	I	ii	IV	V	V7	vi
D	2	3	3	1	1	2
A	0	1	1	2	2	1
D	0	1	0	4	3	0
D	2	3	3	4	6+	2
A	3	4	3	4	6	3
D	4	5	5	6+	4	5
D	4	5	5	6+	6+	5
A	5	6	6	7	6	5
D	7	8	7	8	8	7

Hurree, Hooroo

with optional accompaniment

Mixolydian Mode (DAD)

Scottish Traditional

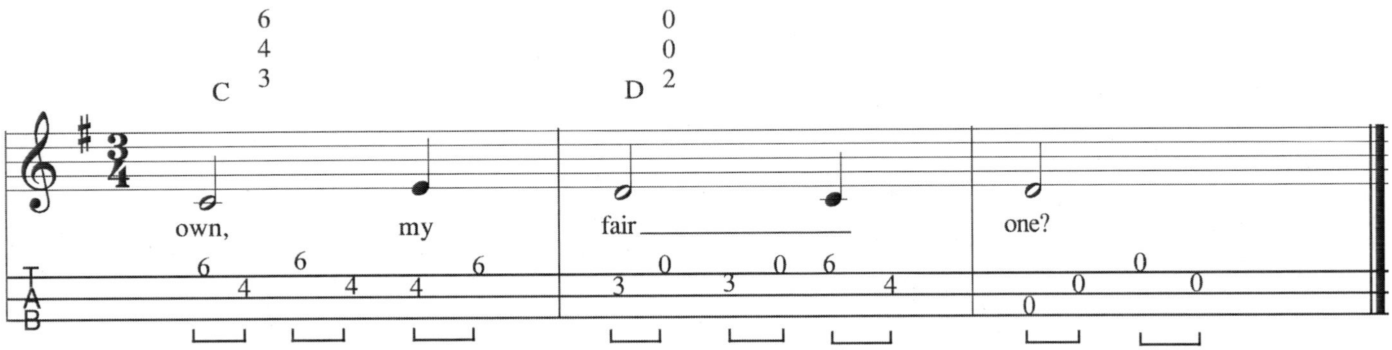

Smiling the land,
Smiling the sea,
Sweet was the smell of the heather,
Would we were yonder just you and me
The two of us together.

All the day long
Out by the peat,
Then by the shore in the gloaming,
Tripping it lightly with dancing
then we together roaming.

Rock-A-My Soul

Mixolydian Mode (DAD)

Spiritual

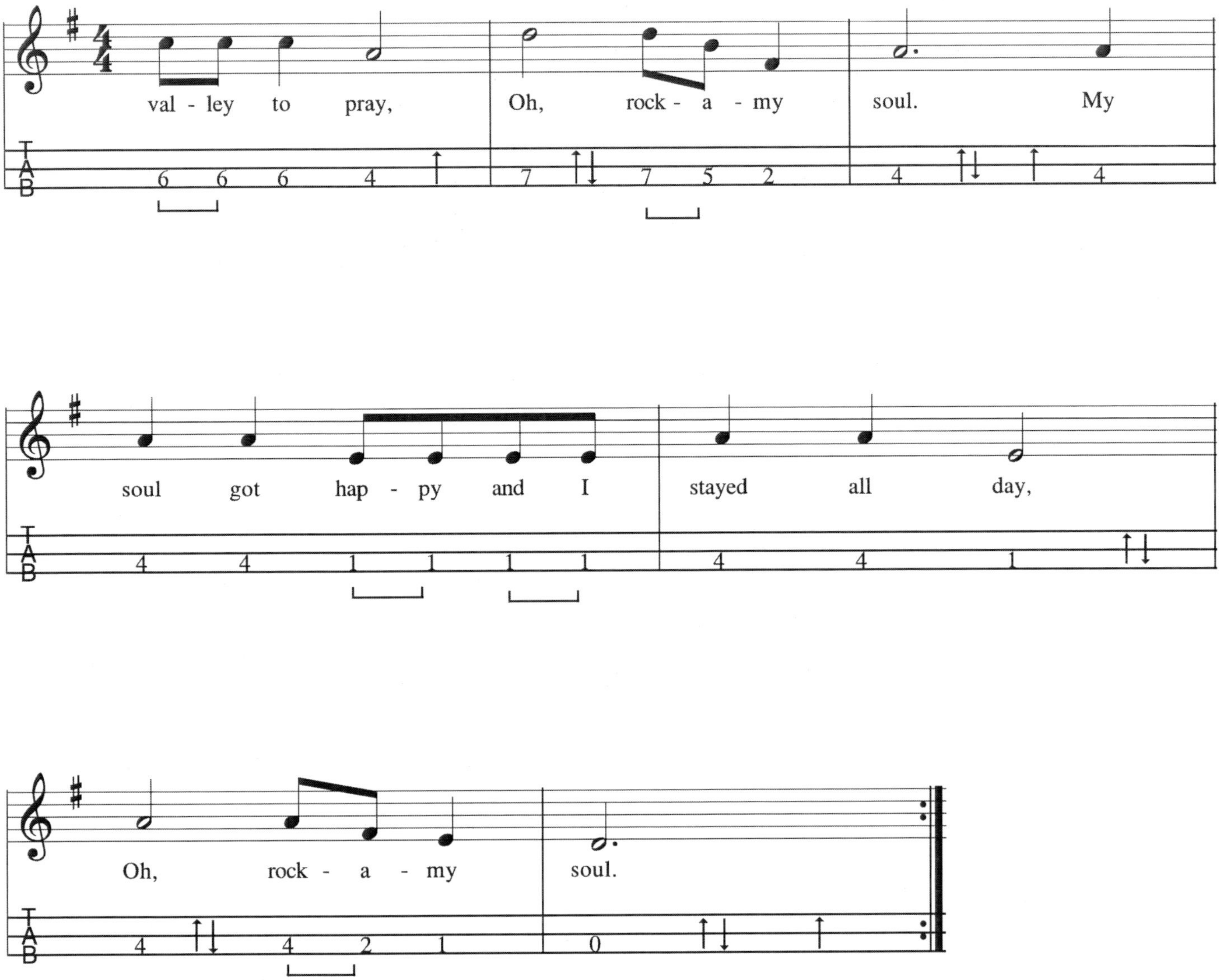

When I was a mourner just like you,
O, rock-a-my-soul,
I mourned and mourned til I came through,
O, rock-a-my-soul.

Rock-A-My Soul

Optional Arrangement

Mixolydian Mode (DAD)

Spiritual

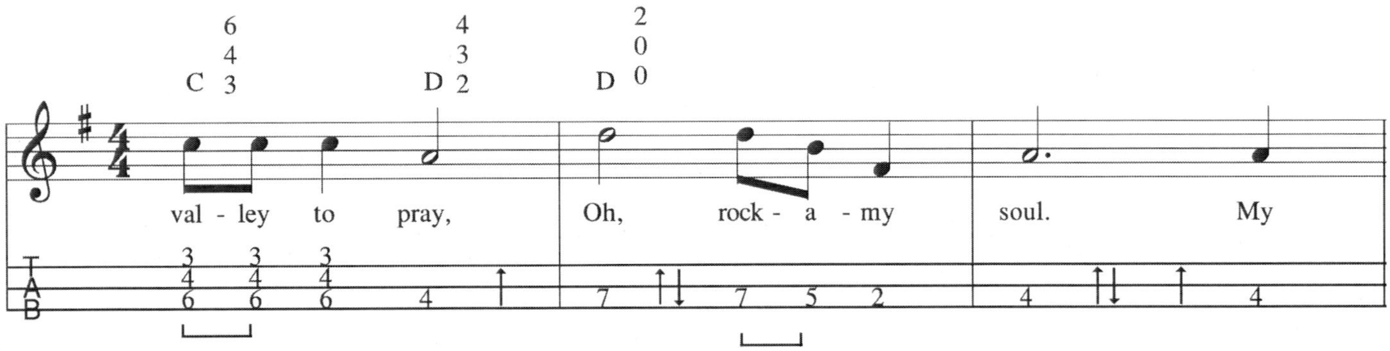

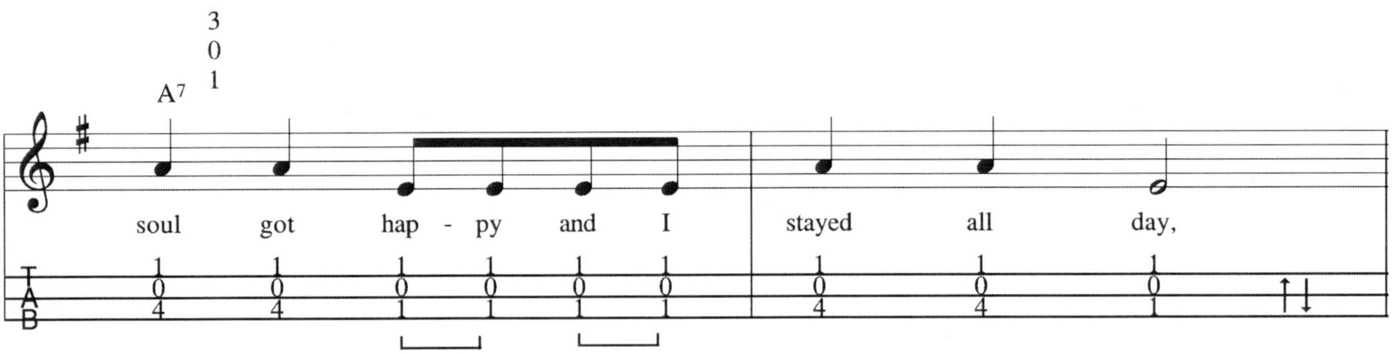

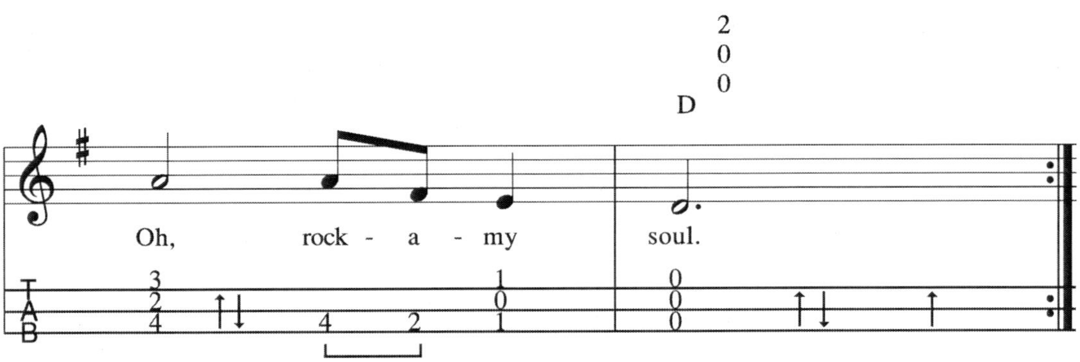

When I was a mourner just like you,
O, rock-a-my-soul,
I mourned and mourned til I came through,
O, rock-a-my-soul.

Little Maggie

with optional accompaniment

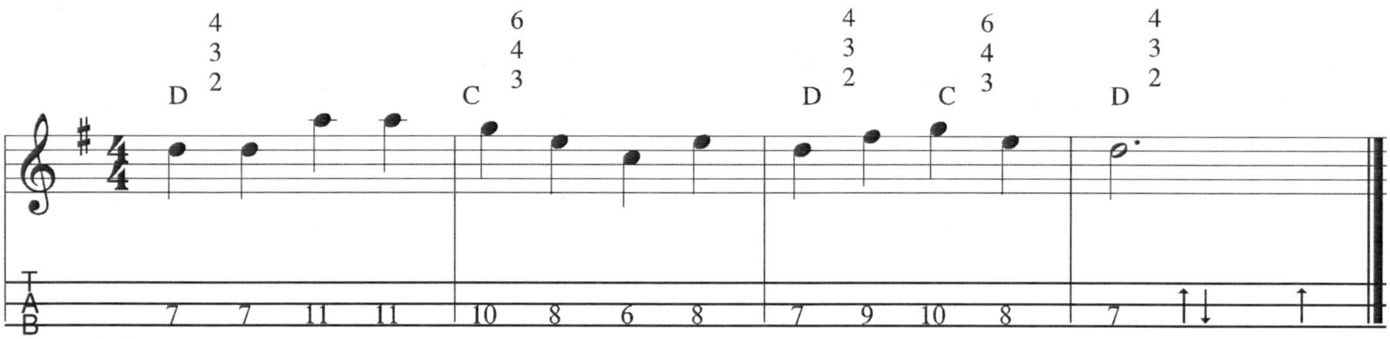

How can I just stand it
To see those two blue eyes.
They're shining like two diamonds,
Two diamonds in the sky.

Pretty flowers were made for bloomin',
Pretty stars were made to shine,
Pretty girls were made for lovin',
Little Maggie was made to be mine.

Marching down to the station,
Got a suitcase in her hand.
She's going for to leave me,
She's bound for some distant land.

Over the Waterfall

Mixolydian Mode (DAD) **Traditional**

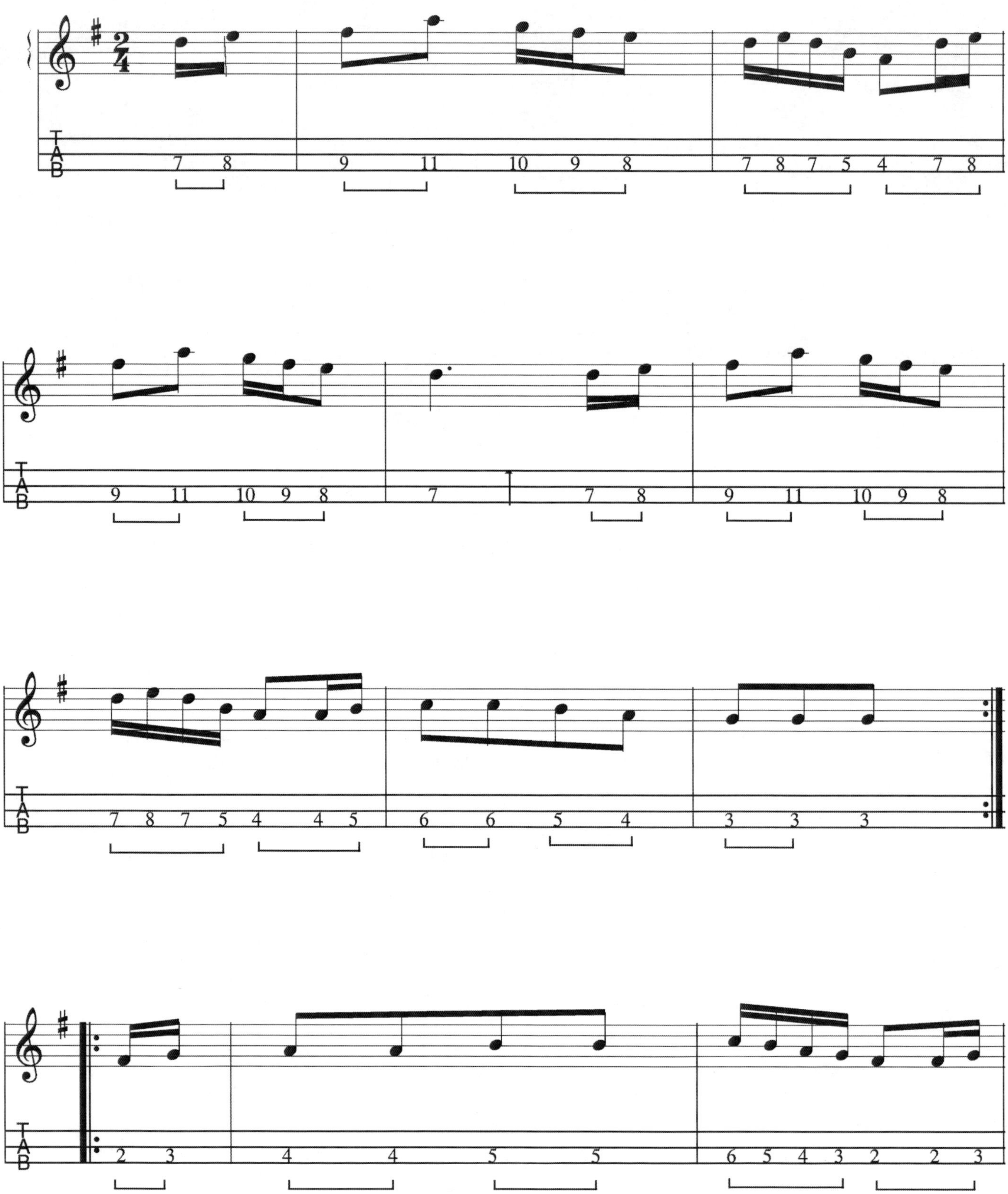

TAB
4 7 6+ 7 8 | 7 2 3 | 4 4 5 5
TAB
6 5 4 3 2 2 3 | 4 0 2 1 | 0

Over the Waterfall

with optional accompaniment

Mixolydian Mode (DAD)

Traditional

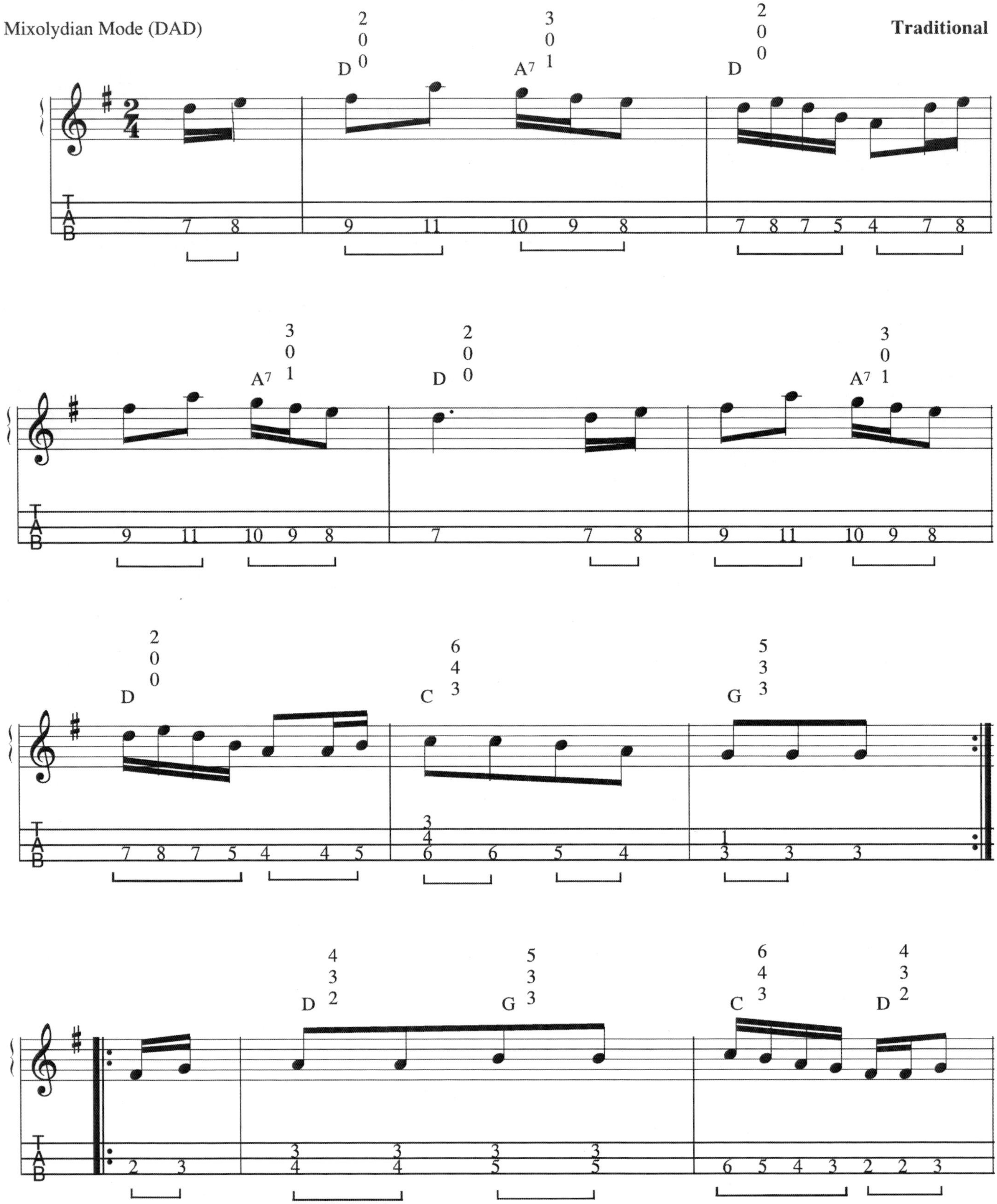

D A D G
C D A D

June Apple

Mixolydian Mode (DAD) **Traditional**

June Apple

Optional Arrangement

Mixolydian Mode (DAD)

Traditional

Aeolian

"Appeasing the tempests of the mind and lulling them asleep"

String Tuning: DAC

1. Fret bass string at fret number 6. Listen to the note and tune the melody string to match that pitch.
2. The scale is found between frets 1 and 8 on the melody string.

ACCOMPANYING CHORD POSITIONS IN DAC SONG SECTION

Dm	Gm	F	A	Am	C
0	0	4	4	4	3
0	3	0	2	4	4
1	4	3	2	0	0

DAC TUNING

	Dm	F	Gm	Am	A	C
	i	III	iv	v	V	VII
D	0	4	3	1	4	3
A	0	0	3	0	2	4
C	3	3	6	0	2	0
D	4	6	7	4	6+	8
A	3	0	6	4	7	6
C	3	3	6	0	9	7
D	7	6	10	8	11	13
A	7	7	10	7	7	11
C	10	10	13	7	9	11

The Butcher Boy

Aeolian Mode (DAC)

Traditional

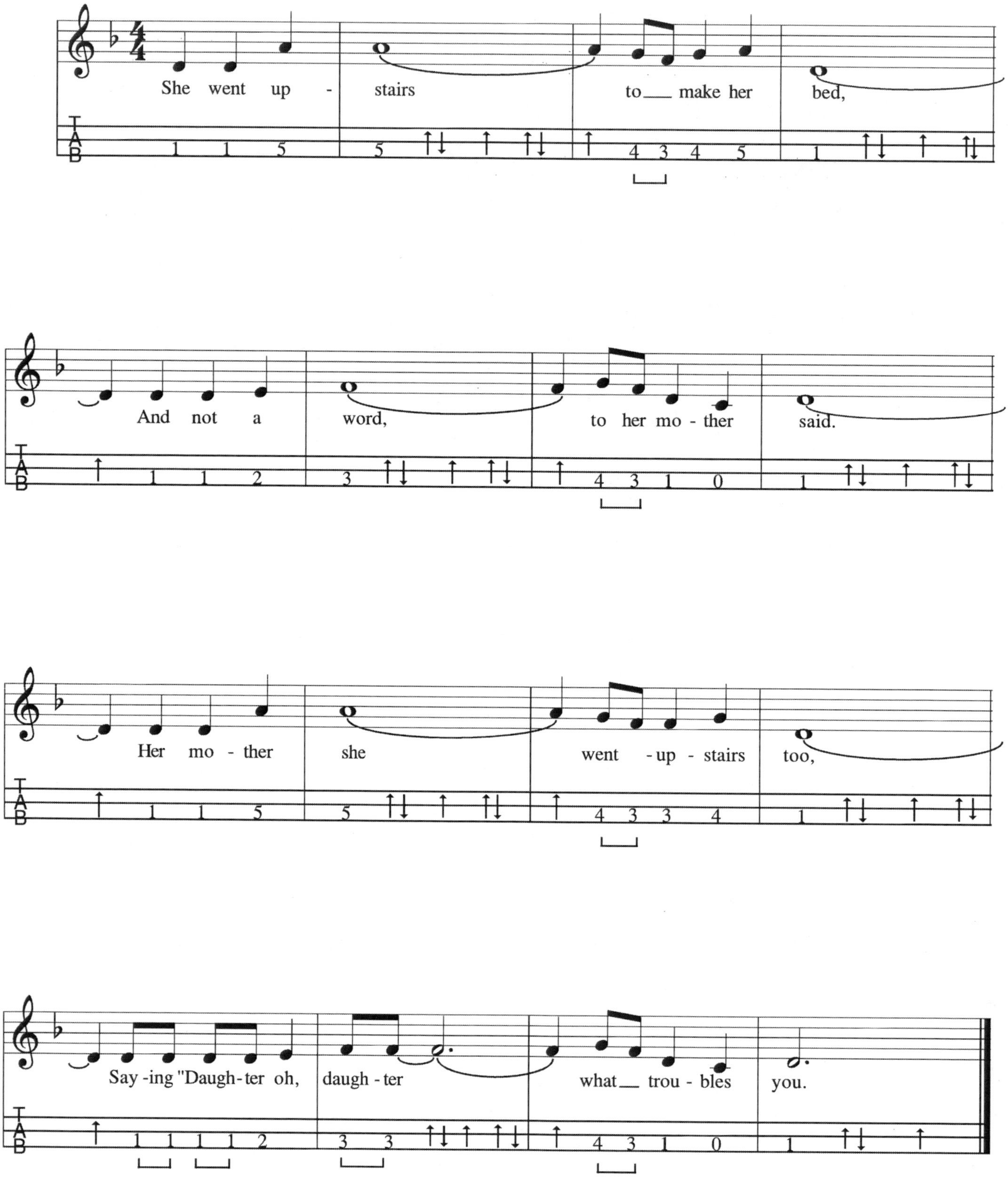

The Butcher Boy

with optional accompaniment

Aeolian Mode (DAC)

Traditional

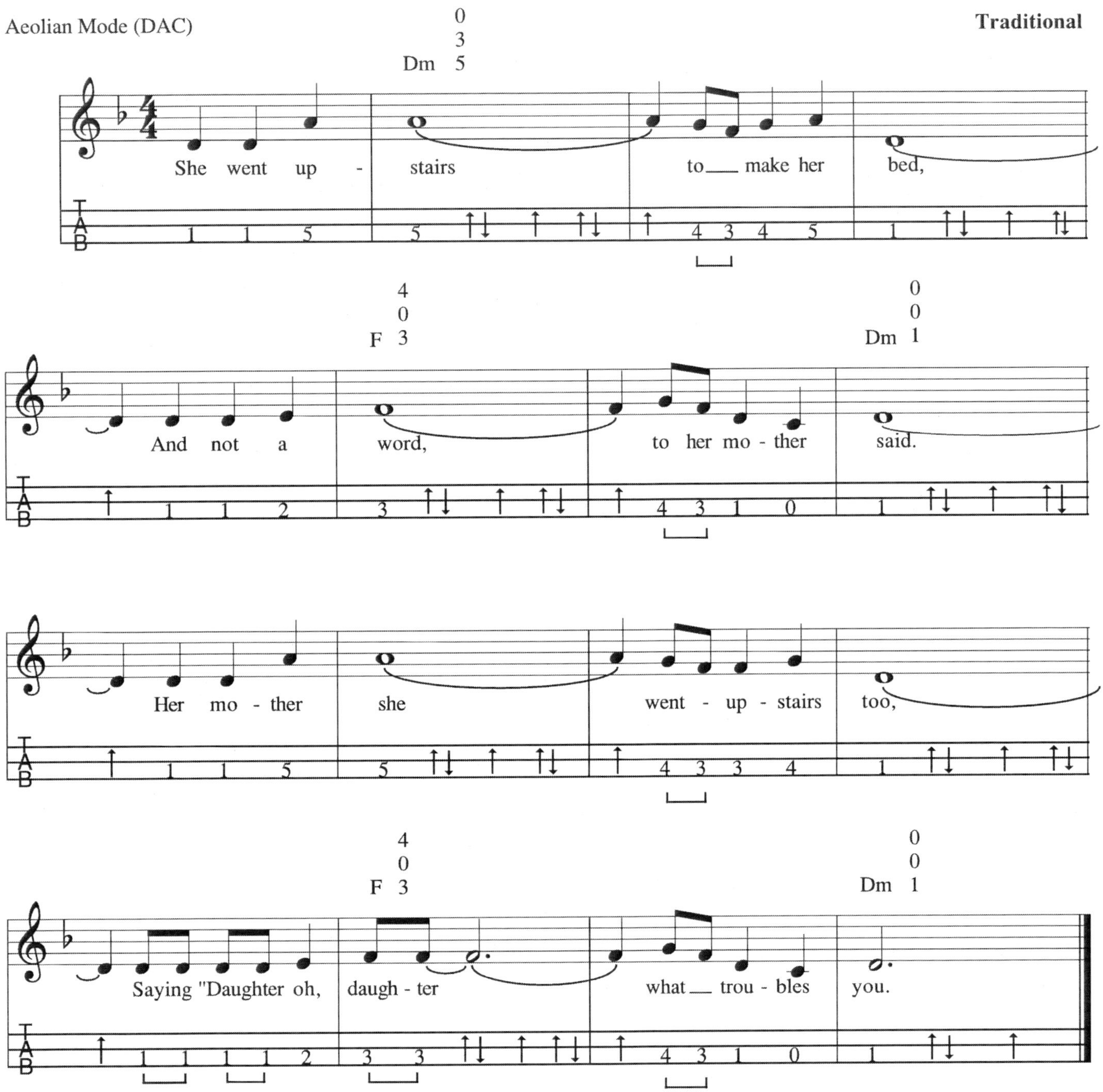

"Oh Mother, oh Mother, I cannot tell
That butcher boy, I love so well,
He courted me my life away,
And now at home, he will not stay."

There is a place in London Town,
Where that butcher boy goes and he sits down.
He takes that strange girl on his knee,
And tell her what he won't tell me.

Her father he came home from work
Saying, "where is daughter, she seems so hurt?
He went upstairs to give her hope,
And found her hanging from a rope.

He took his knife and cut her down,
And in her bosom these words he found:
"go dig my grave both wide and deep
place a marble slab at my head and feet.

And over my coffin place a snow-white dove, To warn the world I died of love.

Nine Hundred Miles

with optional accompaniment

Aeolian Mode (DAC)

Traditional

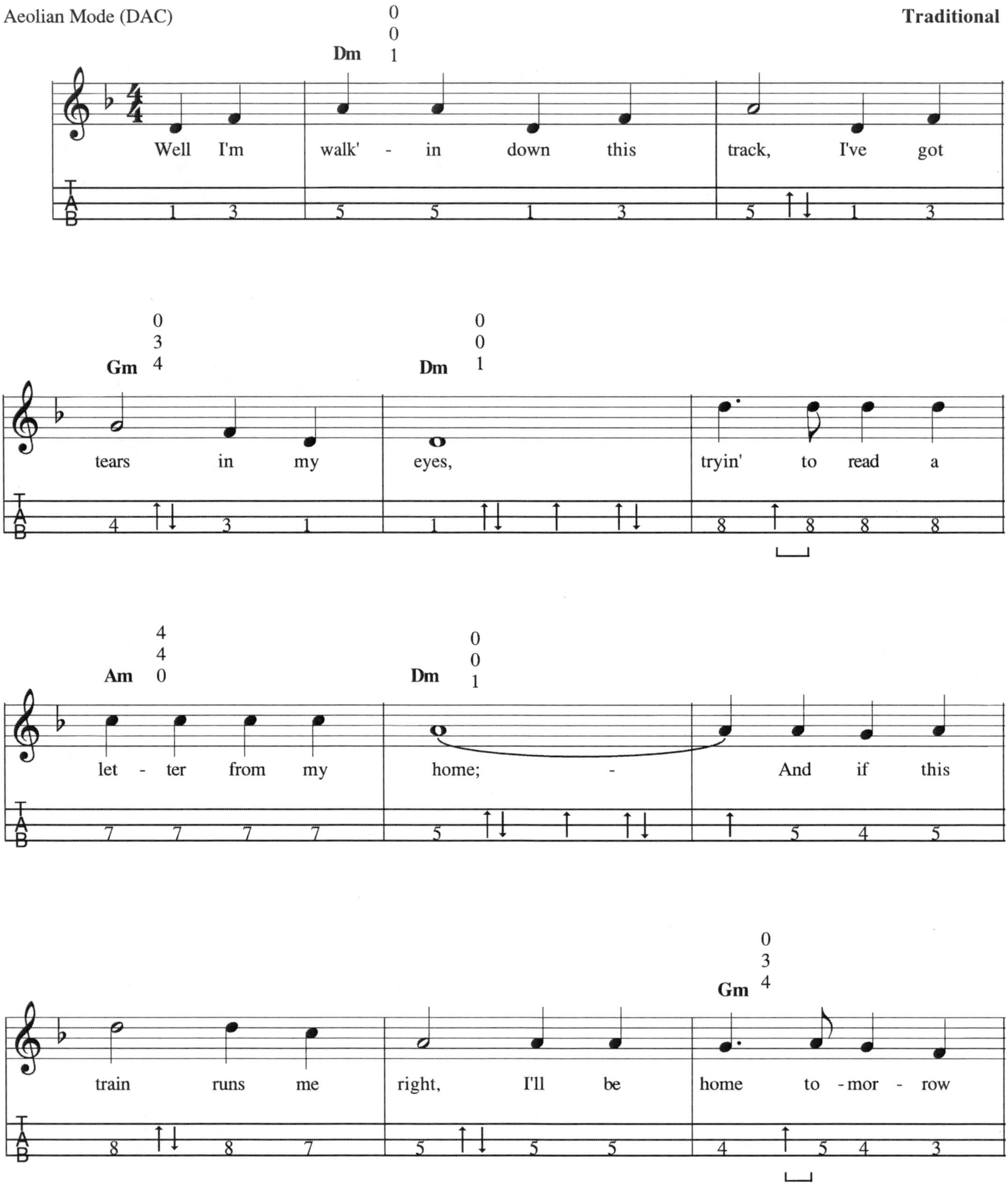

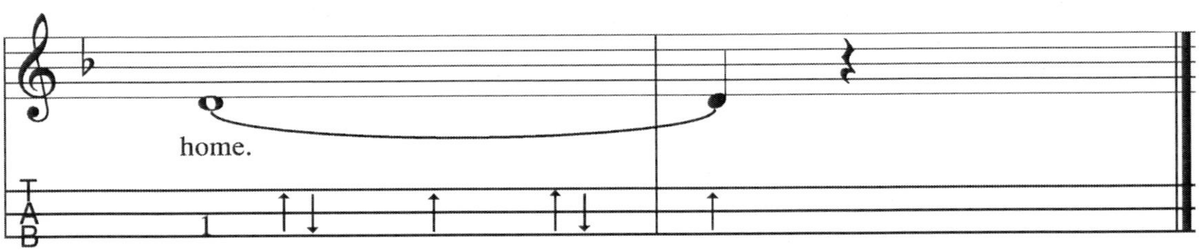

*This song is also known as Reuben's Train.

Wayfarin' Stranger

with optional accompaniment

Aeolian Mode (DAC)

Traditional

Dm
I'm go - ing there to see my
Gm
moth - er To see her there, no more to
Dm
roam. She's wait - ing there right o - ver
Gm
Jor - dan I'm go - ing there, I'm go - ing
Dm
home.

Bound For The Promised Land

Aeolian Mode (DAC)

Southern Gospel

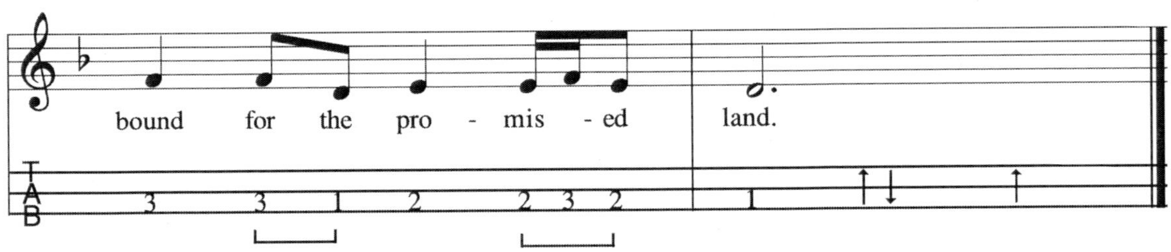

And when I reach that happy land,
I'll be forever blessed.
My Lord will lead me by thy hand
To my eternal rest.

I am bound for the promised land,
I'm bound for the promised land,
Oh, who will go and come with me,
I am bound for the promised land.

Bound For The Promised Land

Optional Arrangement

Aeolian Mode (DAC)

Southern Gospel

And when I reach that happy land,
I'll be forever blessed.
My Lord will lead me by thy hand
To my eternal rest.

I am bound for the promised land,
I'm bound for the promised land,
Oh, who will go and come with me,
I am bound for the promised land.

Shady Grove

Aeolian Mode (DAC) **Traditional**

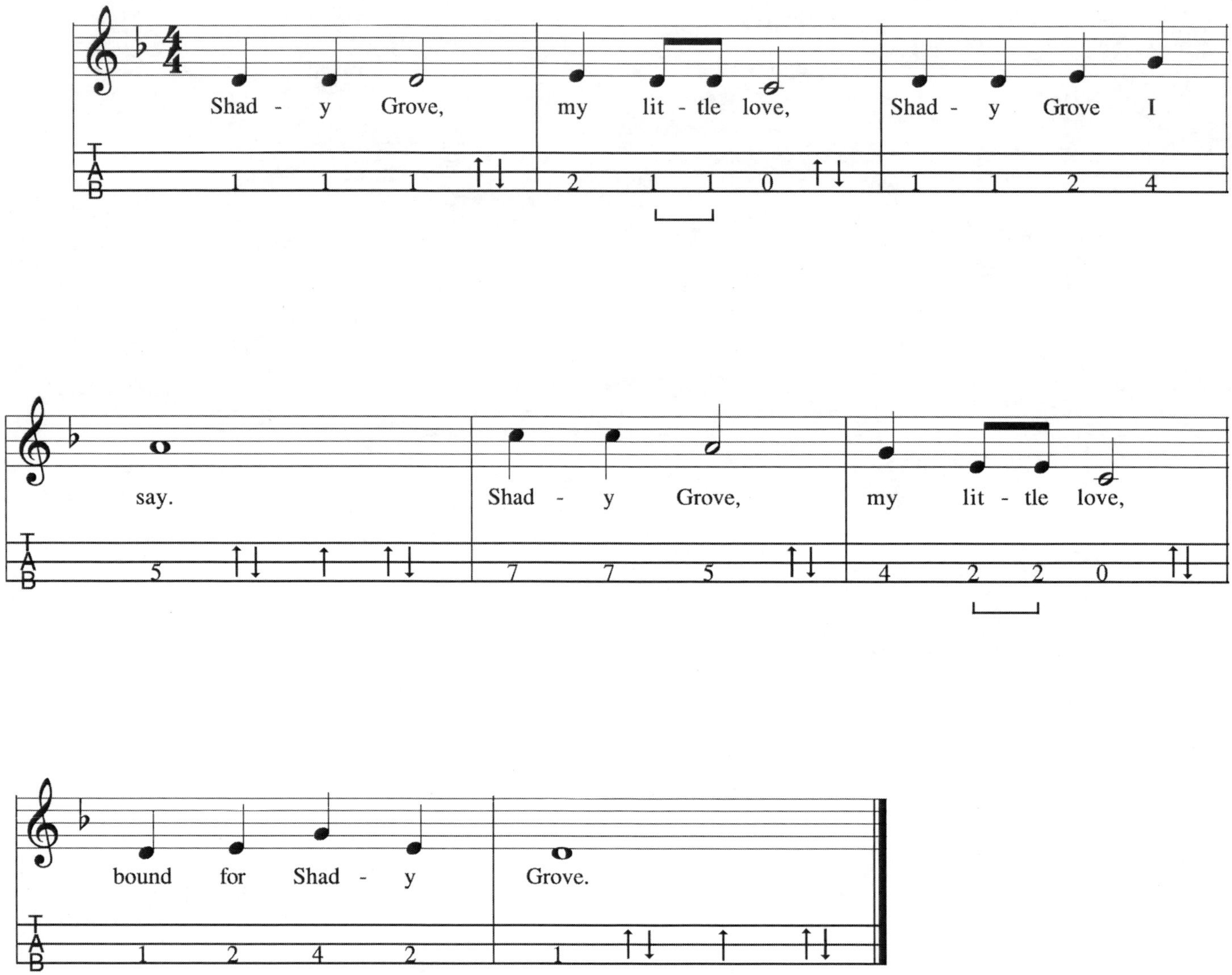

Wish I was in Shady Grove,
Sittin' in a rockin' chair,
And if those blues would bother me,
I'd rock away from there.

When I was in Shady Grove,
Heard them pretty birds sing,
The next time I go to Shady Grove,
Take along a diamond ring.

Shady Grove

with optional accompaniment

Aeolian Mode (DAC)

Traditional

Wish I was in Shady Grove,
Sittin' in a rockin' chair,
And if those blues would bother me,
I'd rock away from there.

When I was in Shady Grove,
Heard them pretty birds sing,
The next time I go to Shady Grove,
Take along a diamond ring.

ALPHABETICAL INDEX

Note-Strum Equivalents

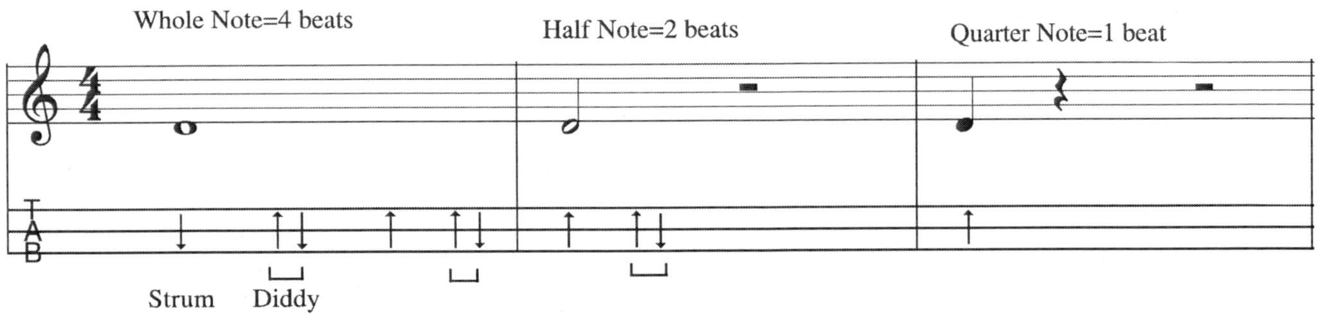

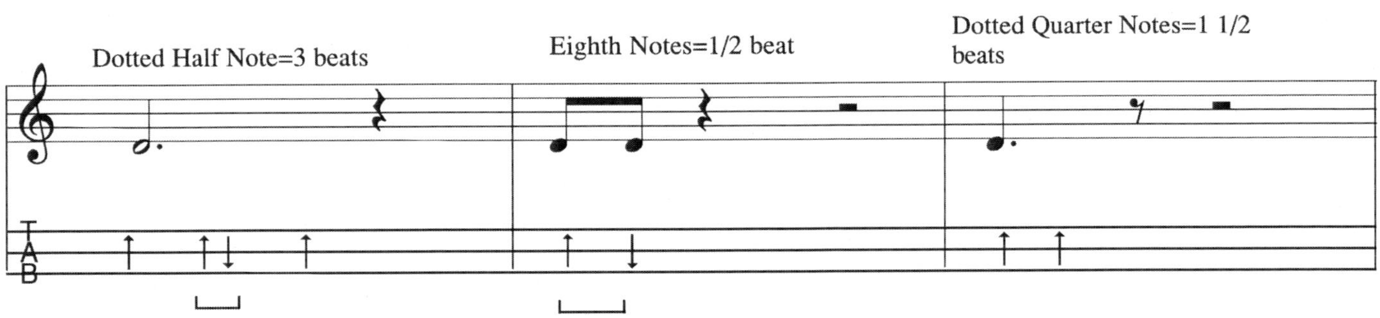

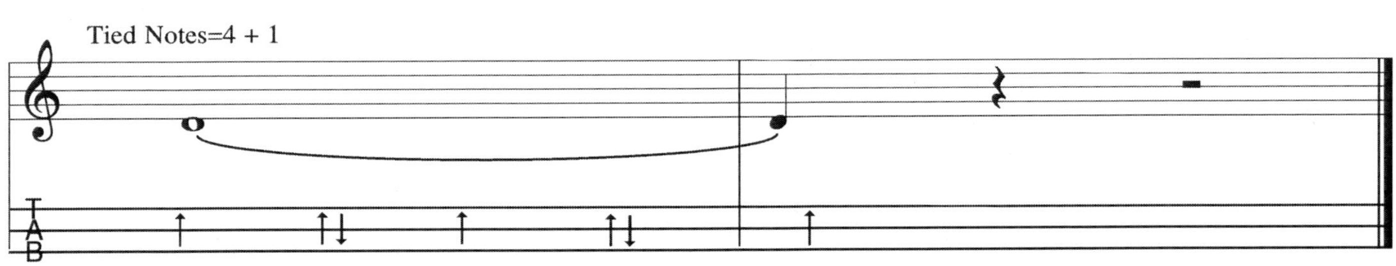

About the Author

Lorinda Jones is a nationally known mountain dulcimer performer and teacher, specializing in both Celtic and American traditional music. She began writing instructional books and tablature in an attempt to meet the needs of the children and adults she taught in schools and workshops across the U.S. She has also organized a regional dulcimer club, Lorinda teaches and performs on other instruments including the Celtic harp, tin whistle, autoharp, guitar, psaltery, piano, and oboe, all of which can be heard on her CD recordings, (*Night Cap, Midwinter's Feast, Cottages & Castles, and No Shadows*). She is also featured on Michael Shull's *Great Players of the Mountain Dulcimer* CD recording. Her belief that music has the power to touch everyone, prompted Lorinda to pursue a second career as a board-certified music therapist, working with children and adults who have mental, emotional, and physical disabilities. She can be contacted at:

P.O. Box 123
Rineyville, Kentucky 40162
LosNotes@inifonline.net
www.LosNotes.com

EXCELLENCE IN MUSIC

MEL BAY®

Since 1947